DYKE STRIPPERS

DYKE STRIPPERS

Lesbian Cartoonists A to Z

Edited by Roz Warren

CLEIS PRESS

This book is dedicated to Alison Bechdel

Copyright ©1995 by Roz Warren

All rights reserved. Except for brief passages quoted in newspaper, magazine, radio or television reviews, no part of this book may be reproduced in any form or by any means, electronic or mechanical, including photocopying or recording, or by information storage or retrieval system, without permission in writing from the Publisher.

Published in the United States by Cleis Press Inc., P.O. Box 8933, Pittsburgh, Pennsylvania 15221, and P.O. Box 14684, San Francisco, California 94114.

Book design and production: Pete Ivey
Cover illustration: Diane DiMassa
Cleis logo art: Juana Alicia

Printed in the United States.
First Edition.
10 9 8 7 6 5 4 3 2 1

Library of Congress Cataloging-in-Publication Data:

Dyke strippers: lesbian cartoonists A to Z / edited by Roz Warren. -- 1st ed.
   p. cm.
   Includes bibliographical references.
   ISBN: 1-57344-008-6 (trade). -- ISBN: 1-57344-009-4 (cl)
   1. Homosexuality--Comic books, strips, etc. 2. Lesbians--Comic books, strips, etc. 3. Lesbian cartoonists--United States--Biography. I. Warren, Rosalind, 1954–
PN6726.D95   1995
741.5'9'086643--dc20   95-1872
                                       CIP

ACKNOWLEDGMENTS

Special thanks to: Nikki Gosch, Toni Armstrong, Jr., Jen Camper, Joan Hilty, Dianne Reum, Alison Bechdel, Kris Kovick, Diane DiMassa, Robin Bernstein, Laurie Kimbrough, Elena Bouvier, and my fabulous editors at Cleis.

The usual heartfelt thanks to: Rick, Tom, Deek, Larry, Isaac, Amy, Beth, Ann, Dad, Hatch, JD, Maggee, and all my pals in the AOL writers' club.

A great big kick in the butt to: Newt Gingrich and Jesse Helms.

PERMISSIONS

Material included in *Dyke Strippers* has also previously appeared in the magazines and periodicals listed in the Resources section. All cartoons are copyright © by their owners unless otherwise noted below.

"Literary Dykes to Watch Out For" from *Dykes to Watch Out For* ©1986 by Alison Bechdel. "Sodomy Blues" and "No Sex" from *More Dykes to Watch Out For* ©1988 by Alison Bechdel. "The Interrogation" (#37) and "Breaking Point" (#66) from *New, Improved! Dykes to Watch Out For* ©1990 by Alison Bechdel. "Union Maids" (#105) and "Support Group" (#113) from *Dykes to Watch Out For: The Sequel* ©1992 by Alison Bechdel. "2 Minds" (#158) and "Nocturne for Diverse Instruments" (#168) from *Spawn of Dykes to Watch Out For* ©1993 by Alison Bechdel. "Lost in Paradise" (#192) from *Unnatural Dykes to Watch Out For* ©1995 by Alison Bechdel. Reprinted by permission of Firebrand Books, Ithaca, New York.

Cartoons by Jane Caminos from *That's Ms. Bulldyke to You, Charlie!* ©1992 by Jane Caminos. Reprinted by permission of Madwoman Press.

Cartoons by Jen Camper from *Rude Girls and Dangerous Women* ©1994 by Jennifer Camper. Reprinted by permission of the artist.

Cartoons by Rhonda Dicksion from *Stay Tooned* ©1993 by Rhonda Dicksion. Reprinted by permission of the artist and The Naiad Press, Inc.

Cartoons by Diane DiMassa from *Hothead Paisan: Homicidal Lesbian Terrorist* ©1993 by Diane DiMassa and Giant Ass Publishing. Reprinted by permission of Cleis Press.

Material from *Tomato* ©1994 by Ellen Forney. Reprinted by permission of the artist.

Material from *A Bitch is Born* and *Bitchy Bitch* ©1991, 1992 and 1994 by Roberta Gregory. Reprinted by permission of the artist.

Material from *What I Love about Lesbian Politics Is Arguing with People I Agree With* ©1991 by Kris Kovick. Reprinted with permission of the artist.

Cartoons by Andrea Natalie from *The Night Audrey's Vibrator Spoke* and *Rubyfruit Mountain* ©1992 and 1993 by Andrea Natalie. Reprinted by permission of Cleis Press.

"Interview with Alison Bechdel" ©1992 by Katie Brown first appeared in *Deneuve*. Reprinted by permission of the author. "Interview with Diane DiMassa" ©1994 by Elana Bouvier first aired on *Amazon Country*, WXPN-FM, Philadelphia. Published by permission of Elana Bouvier. "Interview with Hothead and Chicken" first appeared in *Brat Attack* ©1992 by Fish and Diane DiMassa. Reprinted by permission of the creators. "Interview with Andrea Natalie" and "Interview with Roberta Gregory" ©1993 and1994 by Robin Bernstein first appeared in *The Washington Blade*. Reprinted with the permission of the author and the *Blade*. "Interview with Kris Kovick" ©1993 by Emily Greenberg first appeared in *The Lesbian Center Community News*, Seattle. Reprinted by permission of the author. "Interview with Noreen Stevens" ©1992 by Naomi Guilbert first appeared in *The Uniter*. Reprinted by permission of the author.

CONTENTS

Introduction 7
Alison Bechdel 9
Katie Brown interviews Alison Bechdel 20
Angela Bocage 23
Paige Braddock 27
Jane Caminos 30
Jennifer Camper 33
Roz Warren interviews Jennifer Camper 41
Rona Chadwick 44
Kate DeBold 47
Rhonda Dicksion 49
Diane DiMassa 51
Elana Bouvier interviews Diane DiMassa 60
Wendy Eastwood 63
Leslie Ewing 67
Karen Favreau 70
Nicole Ferentz 72
Fish 74
Fish interviews Hothead and Chicken 84
Ellen Forney 88
Leanne Franson 99
Nikki Gosch 104

Roberta Gregory 106
Robin Bernstein interviews Roberta Gregory 116
Joan Hilty 118
Cath Jackson 130
Kris Kovick 132
Emily Greenberg interviews Kris Kovick 144
Erica Lopez 146
Beck Main 149
Andrea Natalie 152
Robin Bernstein interviews Andrea Natalie ... 157
Jo Nesbitt 159
Barbary O'Brien 161
Michelle Rau 164
Dianne Reum 166
Ursula Roma 176
Noreen Stevens 179
Naomi Guilbert interviews Noreen Stevens 186
T. O. Sylvester 189
Jackie Urbanovic 192
Linda Sue Welch 198
zana 200
Zora 203
Resources and Recommended Reading 205

INTRODUCTION

I decided to put *Dyke Strippers* together because, in the course of editing ten women's humor collections, I'd become a fan of many lesbian and bisexual cartoonists that a lot of people didn't seem to know about yet. It's tough to learn about up-and-coming (or even well-established) lesbian and bi cartoonists because they are, for the most part, published mostly in regional gay and lesbian papers. The good news is that with the growth of cartoon-friendly national publications like *Lesbian Contradiction* and *Deneuve* and Canada's *OH...*, this is changing. Plus "mainstream" venues like *The Funny Times* have begun to welcome the work of cartoonists like Alison Bechdel, Jen Camper, Andrea Natalie and others. Still, this book is the first opportunity most readers will have to enjoy the work of so many talented lesbian and bi cartoonists who are currently cartooning.

There's nothing like being able to phone a cartoonist whose work you love, and have a long, interesting conversation about her art and her life. I hope that reading this book will be the next best thing.

Roz Warren
February 1995

ALISON BECHDEL

"Dykes to Watch Out For"
Duxbury, Vermont

Alison Bechdel began drawing "dykes to watch out for" in letters to friends over a decade ago. Her friends encouraged her to submit her work to *Womanews*, then New York's feminist newspaper, which began running the strip "Dykes to Watch Out For" in 1983. Now, with six collections of the strip in print, Alison's a lesbian icon. (Fellow lesbian icon Diane DiMassa respectfully calls Alison "Your Majesty.")

Over forty papers in the U.S., Canada, and the U.K. currently carry Alison's bi-weekly strip. Most are gay and lesbian, but "Dykes" has also crossed over into mainstream venues like *The Funny Times*. Not that crossing over was ever a goal for Bechdel. In 1994, Universal Press Syndicate (the folks who bring you "Cathy") offered her the unprecedented opportunity to develop a gay strip for the mainstream daily newspapers. She turned them down! "It would have been a whole different career path," she explained in a *Hotwire* interview, "and I'm happy with what I'm doing now. There are cartoonists out there who have a desire to speak to the mainstream; I don't really. I think they should get the chance."

Bechdel *would* like to see her cartoons animated, and she plans a graphic novel about her childhood. But her primary goal, she says, is "to keep drawing 'Dykes to Watch Out For' until I keel over."

Books: *Dykes to Watch Out For, More Dykes to Watch Out For, New Improved! Dykes to Watch Out For, Dykes to Watch Out For: The Sequel, Spawn of Dykes to Watch Out For, Unnatural Dykes to Watch Out For, Gay Comics* all-Alison issue.

Periodicals: *Ms., The Washington Blade, Real Girl, Bay Times* (San Francisco), *Wimmen's Comix, Gay Comics, The Village Voice, off our backs*.

Collections: *Women's Glib, Women's Glibber, What Is This Thing Called Sex?, The Best Contemporary Women's Humor*.

Also available: Annual calendar, t-shirts, mugs, slide-show, postcards.

Birthplace: Lockhaven, Pennsylvania.

Education: Oberlin College.

Creative/Artistic Influences: Dr. Seuss, Richard Scarry, Edward Gorey, MAD, Norman Rockwell, Edward Lear, Jane Austen, Herge R. Crumb, Howard Cruse.

Personal/Political Influences: The lesbian plumber on *Green Acres*, various ex-girlfriends.

Day Job: I haven't had to work another job since 1990.

Procrastination Techniques: Compulsive organizing, *Mary Tyler Moore* reruns.

Pets: My cat.

Activities Undertaken to Unwind: Lawn-mowing, snow-shoveling, recycling.

Most Recent Accomplishment: I quit therapy.

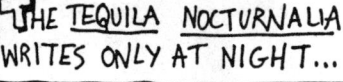

This is a very early Mo strip. I think it's very sexy in a repressed kind of way.

Dykes to Watch Out For

I hadn't really gotten very intimate with any of my characters before this strip. Showing such a dramatic, emotional exchange between Clarice and Toni was a big development for me.

Dykes to Watch Out For

I got an unusual amount of feedback when this strip first came out. Lots of people seemed to identify with it—especially the panel where Mo dumps her recycling into the trash can.

ALISON BECHDEL

This kind of self-referential cartoon always seemed narcissistic to me, because it's more about the comic strip than about the characters. I finally tried it once when I couldn't think of anything else to write about, and it's turned out to be a big reader favorite.

Dykes To Watch Out For

This is one of the first strips I drew with an artist's nib.
Up until this point, I had only drawn with mechanical pens.

Dykes To Watch Out For

I like this strip because it has these long, sweeping panels of activity, like a tracking shot in an Altman film.

Alison Bechdel

Dykes To Watch Out For

This is one of my few strips ever to be censored by a newspaper.

Dykes To Watch Out For

This strip is unusual because I situated my characters in an actual, real-life event—the International Dyke March in New York City. My characters interact with real women I saw at the March.

AN INTERVIEW WITH ALISON BECHDEL

by Katie Brown

"People often ask me when did I become a cartoonist, and I generally give them the answer that I give people who ask when I became a lesbian, and that is that I was born that way," says Bechdel, whose "Dykes to Watch Out For" comic strip reflects our lives and models a utopian lesbian community. "I've always been a lesbian. I've always been a cartoonist."

Ah, but she hasn't always been a lesbian cartoonist. Until graduating from college and hitting on the idea of drawing lesbians, Bechdel drew exclusively men.

Men? Alison Bechdel, who never draws a man unless he's a bewildered dad or a gruff delivery man chomping a stogie, used to draw only men? Yup. As a child, she drew sword fighters, pilots, and average guys in all sorts of settings. Later she drew effeminate, genderbender men in homo-erotic circumstances. But she never drew women.

"It used to bother me a lot," she says. "Not so much when I was a little kid, but when I got older. I thought I had some kind of weird psychosexual disorder. Ultimately, the reason why I was only drawing men *was* because of a psychosexual disorder."

Ba-dum-dum, you think.

"Not mine," she counters. "But our culture's. One of the most insidious ways that misogyny gets expressed in the world is the treatment of women as something other than human beings. Like there are people and there are female people. It's easy to see that in cartoons. The female cat [in the cartoon 'Garfield'] has weird human lips and eyelashes. Or there's the drag queen effect of Minnie Mouse looking like Mickey in a dress and falsies."

But what about all the men this lesbian icon drew? It's not surprising, really. Growing up, Bechdel says, there were no women role models in fantasy or cartoons.

"Look at *Wind In the Willows*, or *The Hobbit*, or *Winnie the Pooh*, or *Peter Pan*, [stories in which] there are no female characters, or there's [just] one. Like Kanga in *Winnie the Pooh*, or Wendy in *Peter Pan*. It's one woman in a sexual role," Bechdel says.

Bechdel didn't like being a girl as a child; she refused to consider herself a girl, and she cites the absence of strong female images as the reason. "As a kid, I was outraged by this gap in the system," she says. "And the way I dealt with it was to disassociate myself from being a girl. To be a girl seemed like the worst, most humiliating thing in the world. I thought of myself as something else—neither a boy nor a girl."

Bechdel enjoys showing audiences what appears to be a photo of four little seven-year-old boys. Turns out, it's a picture of three little boys and one little Alison. There she is, squatting on the front porch stoop, dressed in dungarees, ratty sneakers and a well-worn t-shirt looking for all the world like her male buddies perched next to her.

Then came the day in her junior year of college that she realized she was a lesbian, which awakened her to a greater truth: "That must mean I'm a woman, then," Bechdel recalls she acknowledged with surprise.

Suddenly, now as a lesbian and a woman, Bechdel opened herself to understanding the institutionalized oppression of women, something she had not experienced since she didn't consider herself female. From then on, as a female art major, Bechdel infuriated herself. "I was ideologically opposed to drawing men, but I couldn't draw women," she says.

One long hot day of mindless occupation at a dull summer job, shortly after graduation, Bechdel experienced a brilliant insight: "Why not draw lesbians? It was very awkward at first. Eventually I got the hang of it. But why could I draw a woman if I thought of her as a lesbian? It's probably about self-acceptance. It was safe for me being a woman if I was a lesbian. I was shut off from it for so long because it seemed like such a bum deal to be a girl. Now there was this great deal of being a dyke."

Her ability to draw lesbians, the result of "this great deal of being a dyke," has bestowed upon the lesbian and greater queer community a priceless gift: "Dykes to Watch Out For." The ten-year-old strip is a funny, touching, and loving treatment of our lesbian community through the characters of Mo, Harriet, Clarice, Toni, Lois, Sparrow, Ginger, Jezanna, Thea and their friends. The strip now appears in more than forty lesbian and gay newspapers and alternative papers nationwide, is officially translated into German and surfaces in other bootleg translations, and is collected in six volumes published by Firebrand Books.

Nancy K. Bereano, editor and publisher of Firebrand Books, credits Bechdel's success to her rare talent for using humor to reflect a marginalized population which makes Bechdel a "very loving critic of the lesbian community," Bereano says.

"For a group that is marginal to a larger society to have humor about itself that is pointed but not nasty is very difficult," says Bereano, who started Firebrand in 1985. "The tendency, if you're a cultural group that is apart from the mainstream, whether religious, ethnic or based on sexual orientation, is to internalize the things that the larger culture has said about you. Humor can be very double-edged. It's wonderful to have someone who comes from the lesbian community and is very attached to the lesbian community. Alison has a very big vision. She's not sentimental. She's a real observer, a delightful person."

In the strip, Bechdel addresses misogyny, love, relationships, monogamy, vegetarianism, feminism, animal rights, coming out, the environment, big corporations, activism, civil rights, heterosexism, therapy, commitment, politics, politics, politics, and, uh, politics. Her characters are Latina, African-American, white, Asian, disabled, butch, femme, thin, fat—and they're all feminists. Her community is so varied that *Publisher's Weekly* called "Dykes" "politically correct and racially diverse to a fault." If that's a criticism, it doesn't bother Bechdel.

More importantly to her, Bechdel simply loves drawing her strip. "I love drawing this cartoon," she says in a kind of detached romantic tone. "I love these characters and their world, and I love just picking up my pen and doing the physical drawing."

She speaks with reverence about the women she draws. "I want to draw real women with real bodies and feelings and ideas, women who are adorable, irritating and independent, committed and frazzled. Mostly, I want to draw women who are lovable and who love other women."

That she has fans everywhere she goes is less important to her than the sense of community she shares with her own characters. But having fans is nice.

"It's just an extra benefit that anyone else gets anything out of it," she says. "It's very thrilling. I've gotten letters from women who say, 'I read your comic strip before I met real lesbians.' It served as a kind of temporary community for them. Or that's how they learned the codes, how lesbians look and what they do. I think that's so cool. I got a postcard from this college kid who took a course on lesbian literature at Sarah Lawrence College and learned that most lesbians of generations past—that's you and me—met their first lesbian when they read *The Well of Loneliness*. 'But I met my first lesbian when I read "Dykes to Watch Out For,"' she wrote."

Being a star has been difficult to adjust to, and is very different from her quiet world living alone—and spending a lot of time alone—in a house at the end of a dirt road in a wood in Vermont. Talking about her status as a celebrity icon makes her uncomfortable.

"It's weird, and it's a weird thing to talk about," Bechdel says. "It's a very bizarre experience. But I love it. I totally love that people who don't know me want to know me. It's something I just love, crave and need on some level. I think we all crave attention for who we are and what we do. I actually get it. I never can quite let it in. It'll feel good for ten minutes and then it's, y'know, washing the dishes after the party."

When she's at home in Vermont, she lives with her characters. She talks about them with her friends, and she wonders what they'll do next. She talks about Mo, Clarice, Ginger, Lois and the rest as though they're real people living in real time.

"I feel like ever since I came out, I've been in search of this elusive lesbian community, in which I'd have a close-knit family of friends, be able to walk together, do things together, know everything about one another's lives. I've never found it. My real friends never seem to like each other. Most are caught up in their own projects and ideological differences. Not only is the strip utopian, it's also utopian in that it's a much more cohesive community than I've ever found."

Mo was the first character Bechdel developed, and she readily confesses that she is most like Mo.

"Mo is this young white middle-class dyke vaguely based on me. I was conscious of not drawing her to look like me. I gave her longer hair than me, and glasses. I don't know who I thought I was kidding," says Bechdel, well aware that Mo looks a lot like her, too. "Mo came about naturally. For all practical purposes she is me. She's guilt-ridden, anxious, judgmental, very critical and has very high standards."

Mo even had a role in Bechdel's own break-up with a lover.

"My current ex said to me one day that I was being very critical about something or judgmental—both of them I'm very good at—and she got angry. I said, 'You knew what I was like. You read my comic strip before you met me. Why do you act so shocked when I act like myself?' And she said, 'I thought Mo was a joke. I thought you knew how obnoxious she was.' So, yes, Mo is a joke, but she's real, too."

Ginger is probably Bechdel's favorite character, "if I had to go be on a desert island with one." Ginger is also "how I would like to be if I wasn't so much like Mo."

Fundamentally, all of the characters are somehow related to their creator. "Lois and Sparrow and Ginger are the three housemates. They represent my sensual, spiritual and rational sides. My Lois side has a leather jacket, even though my Mo side disapproves. Sparrow is the part of me that thinks everyone who is not in therapy or on a twelve-step program is addicted and is in denial. Ginger has a tendency to over-intellectualize." Clarice represents Bechdel's efficient side. "She's a very hard worker. She's also kind of a control freak."

Bechdel is involved in their lives in that she draws them, and she has general expectations for story lines. But the strip and the characters take on lives of their own.

"I don't know certain things until I create certain situations and see how they react," Bechdel says. When a character surprises her with a response or an action, "it's such a thrill. When it comes to you, it's better than the best sex ever!"

What Bechdel does have control over is the general story line and the time in which things happen. Now, after nine years of drawing the strip, Bechdel is beginning to worry about the time lapse in the story.

"As the characters are getting to this early-thirties mark, time is becoming more of an issue, which is true for me, too. I'm just suddenly very conscious of the passing of time in a way that I wasn't before. I'm trying to figure out ways to have them age gradually. Looking in the mirror every day, you don't notice how you're aging. So, one thing I'm doing is having Lois change her hair cut. Instead of her flattop, she's growing her hair out. I want to show her changing."

While aging is a new consideration for Bechdel, Toni's and Clarice's new adventure into motherhood is an example of new directions for "Dykes to Watch Out For." "The strip seems to be exploring the subtleties of how these women interact, more of the emotional interchange, more drama as opposed to issues. A lot of my previous stuff was issue-heavy," Bechdel says.

Sometimes Bechdel wonders if she's at risk of losing touch with her audience. Living in the country makes drawing and writing about an urban community a challenge. Sometimes she worries about understanding the dynamics of her younger audience, and sometimes, she even worries about the durability of the strip itself.

"What happens when it's more acceptable to be a lesbian in our culture, which it's becoming more and more," Bechdel asks. "What happens to my strip? Will there still be a need for it? As society becomes more accepting, is our subculture going to disappear? Or will it get co-opted in the way that feminism did?"

No matter what happens to the strip, feminism itself will continue to flow as a force in the story lines and character development. But how feminism is portrayed also takes on importance, particularly where younger audiences are concerned. When Bechdel talks to younger audiences about misogyny and the representation of women in the media, she sometimes feels like she has just plunged into a generation gap. The feminine fashion style adopted by some younger lesbians also unnerves her. "When I talk about Blondie, my whole little rap is about how Blondie is this ultra-feminine cartoon character—and this is how young women are dressing. They don't think anything of it. Then I really feel like a stegosaurus."

Still, Bechdel finds the shift in perception and attitude refreshing—and necessary.

"I think these younger women are instinctively feminist," she says. "Dress is another function of challenging the orthodoxy of feminism. I think it's a sign of strength in our community. Finally, women who don't fit the lesbian army pattern are coming out about it. I felt threatened at first when the whole lipstick thing came into vogue. But I think it's great. It's just more of who we are."

The feminine style is also making its way into "Dykes to Watch Out For." Although Bechdel regards Toni as a femme, the first real femme character, Thea, was introduced last year. Ironically, Thea's character challenged Bechdel's old inability to draw women.

"To draw a lesbian who looks like a straight woman, it's a whole trip," Bechdel laughs.

Bechdel's development as a storyteller, writer, artist and chronicler has also been dramatic. From a technical perspective, Bechdel has matured as an artist, says Firebrand's Bereano. "We used to get stuff on all different kinds of paper, drawn with seventeen different pens. We couldn't get them to register [during printing]. She was new and hadn't thought about that stuff," Bereano says. "Now she's much more sophisticated as a cartoonist, too. The amount of stuff she can get into a single frame is amazing. Years ago she wouldn't have been able to figure it out."

Not only has her skill expanded to drawing "straight-looking" women, Bechdel also has pushed herself to more fully develop her characters of color. Drawing black, Latina and Asian women has been a challenge and a risk.

"There's something kind of arrogant in writing about their lives. I don't know what it's like to be African-American, or Chinese-American, or Latina," Bechdel says. "I don't necessarily know how these women think or feel or respond to various situations. It's just kind of tricky territory. But not having women of color is not the answer. It's important to do it right."

Bereano admires Bechdel's desire to take risks. "She never pretends she's anything other than Alison Bechdel," Bereano says. "I have a couple of black dyke friends who say the stuff is funny to them. Alison is able to get the differences in intonation and presentation in the black characters, so that not all the black characters, or all the white characters, sound alike."

Bechdel will continue taking on new ideas and confronting new situations as long as she perpetuates "Dykes to Watch Out For." And she has no intention of ending the strip or walking out on her characters' lives.

"My fear is that if I ever stopped doing 'Dykes to Watch Out For,' I wouldn't have anything left, that's all I have in me," Bechdel says. "I hope if it's ever time to quit, I'll know it. But my perspective is that I want to do this forever. I want to grow old with these women."

ANGELA BOCAGE

"(Nice Girls Don't Talk About) Sex, Religion and Politics"

San Francisco, California

Angela Bocage created and edits the quarterly anthology *Real Girl*, "the sex comic for all genders and orientations by cartoonists who are good in bed." Her strip, "(Nice Girls Don't Talk About) Sex, Religion and Politics," is self-syndicated nationally through AIDS News Service, where she serves as graphics editor.

A fine arts graduate of UC-Santa Cruz who cites Marcel Duchamp as a major influence, Bocage abandoned her job at a headhunting firm in the mid-eighties to devote herself to cartooning. An active member of the "girl art gang" Not Nice Girls, she helps create cultural events "on the edges of pornography, satire, fashion and politics, by lesbian and bisexual women."

Other central commitments are her two young children Robin and Jasmine, her dear friends, who include *Girljock* cartoonist/editrix Roxxie, and defending full reproductive freedom for women. And, she has a tattoo of Krazy Kat.

Books: *Real Girl* (editor).

Periodicals: *Frighten the Horses, East Bay Guardian, Processed World, Wimmen's Comix, Weird Smut, Gay Comics, Girljock, Lana's World*.

Collections: *Women's Glibber, Choices, Strip AIDS USA*.

Birthplace: Fayetteville, Arkansas.

Influences: Women who smile at me, the Bay Area Coalition for Our Reproductive Rights—fighting for women's health and against racist, misogynist, women-controlling swine since 1988!—Michael Botkins and Steve Finley, my extended family bro's.

Dislikes: Christian Right hate and hubris, so ready and willing to assert itself over women's and children's lives. Some people havin' too much when too many don't have nothin'. The fact that I have to sleep away at least four hours per twenty-four.

Most Recent Accomplishment: Getting into a good law school with a scholarship, doing well, and raising my kids to love themselves and fight the power. Also, I've remembered to wear clothes to school *every day*.

Goals: To become a real good lawyer (for the people!), to meet a girl who looks like Ely at the end of *Go Fish* and talks like a Sarah Schulman character, to continue to wear clothes to school every day.

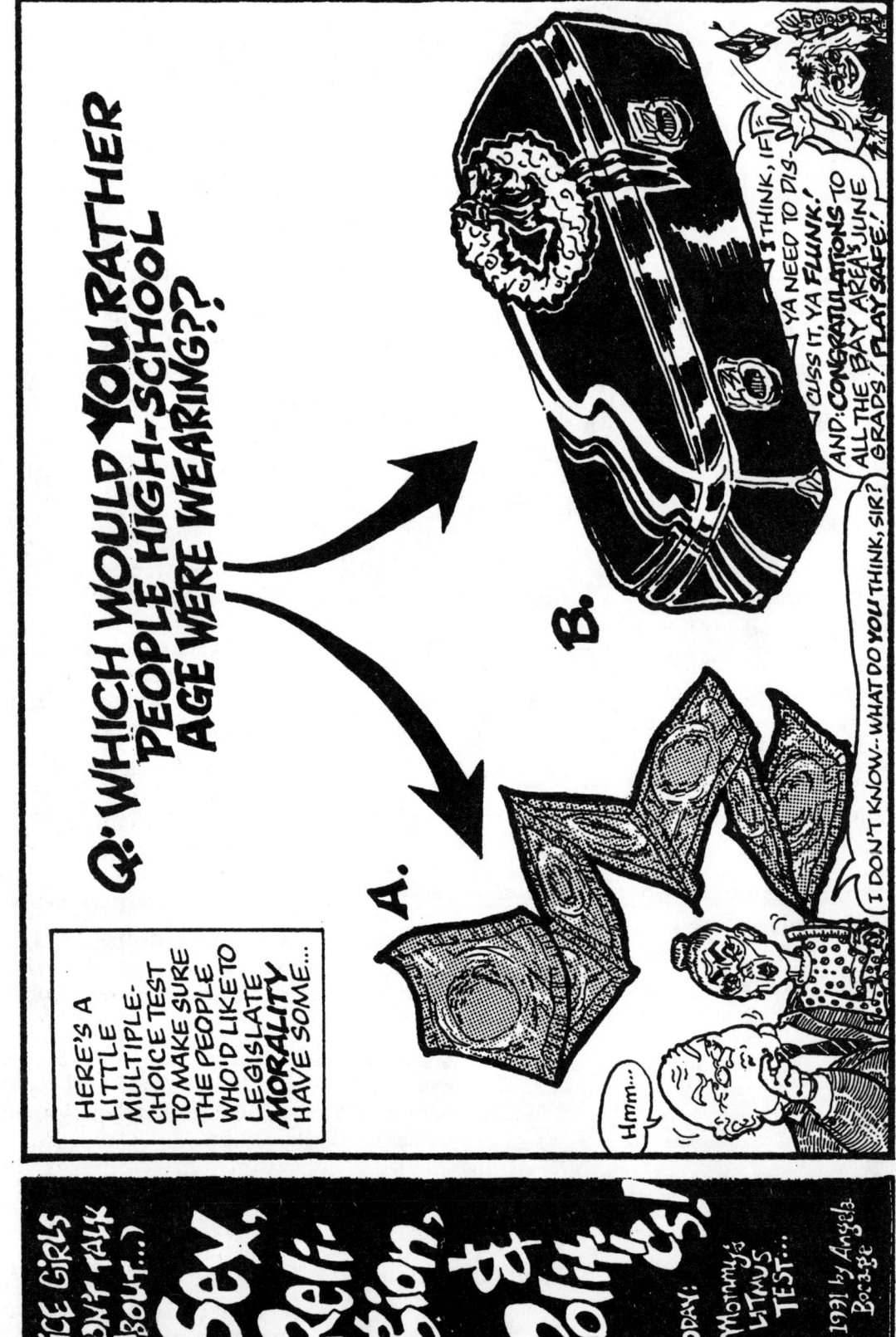

PAIGE BRADDOCK

"See Jane"

Atlanta, Georgia

Paige Braddock works as an illustrator for the news department at *The Atlanta Journal-Constitution*. Addicted to cartooning since age seven, Paige has been working on some form of a comic strip since that time: "I started out tracing pictures of Beetle Bailey out of the Sunday funnies and moved on to create my own long list of short-lived characters." One character, "Sadie," evolved from "the star of a strip set in the wild west. When I got to college, she morphed into a college freshman." The strip ran daily for four years in the University of Texas student newspaper and the *Knoxville Journal*.

Braddock, having firmly established herself in her "day job," is just beginning to refocus on her first love, cartooning. "I'd love to be widely published but I'm not willing to tone down my work so it'll be more marketable for mass consumption," she says. "I recently heard Charles Schultz speak, and his big tip for fellow cartoonists was, 'Write for yourself, write what you think is funny.' And that's what I try to do."

Her one-panel strip "See Jane" grew from the idea that Jane—from the grammar school reader, "See Dick, see Jane, see Spot"—would be a universal character for all women.

Periodicals: *Deneuve, International Comic Strip Pages*.

Collections: *The Best in Diagrammatic Graphics* (B.T. Batsford/London).

Creative Influences: Bill Waterson ("Calvin and Hobbes"), Jeff MacNelly (editorial cartoonist for the *Chicago Tribune*). Both are great illustrators. The guy who drew "Alley Oop" (now retired) took me under his wing when I was in high school and taught me how to lay out and plan a gag, lettering techniques, what kind of paper to use...he even gave me my first quill pen. We still keep in touch.

Dislikes: Cathy Guisewite. Her illustration work is one-dimensional, and the content of her writing is insulting to women. All she ever writes about is dieting, chocolate and her lack of culinary skill. Cartoons ought to be as much about art as about words. You'll find that well-written, horribly drawn cartoons get published, but never the other way around. The drawing should be equal to the story line. In the beginning, great cartoonists like Windsor McCay ("Little Nemo In Slumberland") would take up an entire broadsheet in a Sunday paper with intricate art and a whimsical story. Even Charles Schultz says to learn to draw from life before you attempt to draw cartoons.

Leisure Activities: I have two dogs, Scout, a miniature golden retriever and Rudy, a dachshund. When I'm not playing with them, I'm reading, cruising bookstores and having coffee with friends. I bought a new twenty-seven-inch TV, but find I'm not watching it that often. I'm starting to feel that the bigger the screen, the more brain cells it sucks.

Awards: The Society of Newspaper Design has given me five awards for informational graphics.

Psychobabble for the emotionally impaired

JANE CAMINOS

New York, New York

Jane Caminos was born in 1947 in Brooklyn, an only child, and grew up in Northern New Jersey. "I was head drum majorette, and a clarinet player," she notes. "I wanted to be a Rockette. Still do." She graduated from the Rhode Island School of Design in 1969 and moved to Boston where she began a long, successful career as a designer and illustrator, first in book publishing and later, as an independent. In 1991, she "abandoned ship in search of reality," moving her personal life and her design and illustration studio, Illustratus, to Tribeca in New York City. She continues to illustrate for Fisher Price and for publishers such as Doubleday, Scholastic and Macmillan.

Caminos is also a talented painter who has had numerous one-woman exhibitions of her art. She used to paint "only for relaxation and to combat the rules imposed by commercial work," but in the late eighties, the owner of a gallery in Brookline, Massachusetts convinced her to show her work publicly. Since then, her paintings have been exhibited in galleries and public spaces throughout Eastern Massachusetts and New York.

A separatist when she first came out, the result of being "instructed mercilessly in feminist politics by an initial lover," Caminos eventually "grew bored with the narrow viewpoint, so moderated." Now, she says, "I can be domestic, plus fix the plumbing and wiring, and chop wood." She concludes: "I was a street protester during 'Nam; now I'm a Democrat with a disillusioned cynicism. Same as many of us, I'd wager."

Book: *That's Ms. Bulldyke to You, Charlie!*

Periodicals: *Christopher Street, Gaze Magazine* (Minneapolis), *Lesbians in Colorado, Network Magazine.*

Collections: *What Is This Thing Called Sex?, The Best Contemporary Women's Humor.*

Formative Influences: Thurber since I was three, and later, Don Martin in MAD.

What I Do to Unwind: Indulge in various oral excesses, do the pony, go to hear live music, sit by the Hudson River and look at the horizon, dream of being on the coast of Maine instead of in my dark apartment, meditate, go to sleep to a tape of magnificent thunder storms.

Hobbies/Interests: My mother says my painting is a hobby. This creates a therapy issue, but therapy in NYC is a hundred and twenty dollars an hour, so I keep it as a private hair shirt of resentment. I love to give elaborate dinner parties, keep up with music, buy shoes, glassware and plates. I used to love gardening but NYC makes this an imaginary activity. I sew slipcovers, build furniture, play no sport of any kind.

Relationship: I have a wonderful lover of seven years. Thank God. No need for change, at last.

JENNIFER CAMPER

"Camper"
New York, New York

Jen jokes that she got into cartooning because most of the needed supplies are "small and easy to shoplift." She describes the characters in her multi-panel strip "Camper" as "sexy, streetwise, working-class women. They don't wear Birkenstocks, they wear high-heels or boots. They're not academic either. They just go out and fuck." While some of her cartoons have stirred up some controversy, Jen says, "I never set out to shock people. I draw what I think is funny. I'm just trying to be humorous or to illustrate a scenario that needs visibility."

Much of her work is political. "Naughty Things To Do With Communion Wafers" was initially rejected by two gay newspapers which then published the 'toon to illustrate stories about how Jen's work has been subject to censorship. "I'm very opinionated. I've got something to say about everything, but I never get angry. I just joke. I figured out that I can say anything, as long as I'm smiling."

Book: *Rude Girls and Dangerous Women.*

Periodicals: *The Washington Blade, On Our Backs, The Advocate, Out, Hysteria, Seattle Twist, Milwaukee In Step, Chicago Nightlines, Gay Comics, Real Girl, Dyke's Delight, Wimmen's Comix.*

Collections: *Women's Glib, Women's Glibber, What is This Thing Called Sex?, The Best Contemporary Women's Humor.*

Also available: Postcards.

Birthplace: Madison, Wisconsin.

Formative Influences: Art, books, movies, theater, music, food, sex and nature.

Dislikes: Food with not enough garlic in it.

Leisure Activities: Speeding tickets, inappropriate laughter, sticky substances.

Goals: Euphoria.

Cartoons have such a long tradition of outrageous violence that I was happy to balance the scales with my own version of Wham! Bam! Pow! I'm still surprised that so many men, after eons of dishing it out, really can't take it.

This is one of my all-time favorite cartoons. I think it is very sexy and very lesbian. I can't for the life of me explain why.

Single-panel cartoons, when they're done well, have a pristine perfection. They must say a lot with a bare minimum, much like poetry. This is one of the few single panels I've done that I think works.

In the winter of 1989, AIDS activists entered St. Patrick's Cathedral in New York and disrupted mass to protest the church's statements on AIDS, birth control, lesbians and gays, and women. In the disturbance, some communion wafers either fell or were thrown to the floor. Afterwards, much debate raged as to whether the protesters had gone too far and were insulting the Catholic religion. I found it bizarre that many people seemed to be more upset over the wafers on the floor than over the thousands of deaths from AIDS. "What is it with these wafers?" I thought, and drew this cartoon, over which there was much controversy.

One of the joys of being a cartoonist is that one works with a set of cartooning standards that has somehow evolved through time. There are the conventions of representing time in panels, speech and thought in balloons, and sound effects in weird onomatopoeic words. Symbols are universally agreed upon—certain lines indicate motion, a string of punctuation indicates cursing, and a light bulb appears over the head of a character with an idea. Working with these conventions, cartoonists have the opportunity to bend and twist them. I've drawn a series of cartoons with these two women who not only know that they are characters, they know how to control the cartoon as well.

AN INTERVIEW WITH JENNIFER CAMPER

by Roz Warren

Roz Warren: How did you begin cartooning?

Jen Camper: I always drew pictures and wrote stories and made things, as far back as I can remember. I didn't always call it "art" or "cartoons"—mostly I did it because it was fun, or because it was something I did with my sister and brother or with friends. Humor and satire were a way of life, but when you're a kid it's called goofing off and making fun of people. Once I was in school, and was generally bored to tears, it became a means of survival.

Roz: Can you tell me something about your background? Your family and upbringing? Education?

Jen: I grew up in a family where it was not only okay to be independent, but very much encouraged. My parents are from different backgrounds—my father was Lebanese, intellectual, and politically liberal, and my mother was a bit of a black sheep in a conservative WASP family. Also, my mother is six feet tall and my father is five foot four, something I never found strange. I remember being teased by other kids who said the man should be taller. I thought they were crazy. My parents raised us without organized religion and with very little television, for which I am now thankful. My father was sick for a few years with terminal bone cancer, and died when I was nineteen. Back then, there wasn't much support for terminal patients and their families, and my mother pretty much handled everything herself. My parents and my sister and brother are people I genuinely love and respect—I'm really lucky to come from such a family.

I went to college on an Oscar Mayer Scholarship. My father worked in the meat packing factory, as did my sister and I for a few summers, and the company gave out scholarships to kids with good grades.

Roz: Which gay and lesbian cartoonists were already on the scene in the early eighties when you began publishing your cartoons?

Jen: By that time, the so-called "underground" comics were no longer the exclusive domain of heterosexual white boys. There were comic books like *Tits and Clits*, *Wimmen's Comix*, Roberta Gregory's *Dynamite Damsels*, Mary Wing's *Dyke Shorts*, Trina Robbins' many comic books, and Howard Cruse's *Gay Comics*.

Howard was very encouraging and published my work. He was doing exciting comics himself, and his interest in my cartoons and his more than generous advice and friendship had a profound effect on me and inspired me to continue cartooning. He was responsible for encouraging and publishing a lot of beginning cartoonists and connecting us with each other. To this day he's a great friend and someone I still pester with technical questions and for advice.

Roz: It seems to me that there's a strong feeling of community among lesbian and gay cartoonists. You, Alison, Andrea, Kris and Diane all seem to be aware of and very supportive of each other's work.

Jen: There is a lot of support among lesbian and gay boy cartoonists. Information is shared and advice is given. Maybe it's because cartooning is such a solitary occupation that it makes cartoonists hungry for interaction. Also, there aren't many of us out there, and we all do such different kinds of art, so I don't feel there's much competition—unless there is and I'm just blind to it. I enjoy talking shop with other cartoonists and I love putting together group projects.

Roz: Where did you first publish and what kind of response did you get?

Jen: In the early eighties, I was living in Boston and drew for *Gay Community News*. Those were still the days of volunteers and collectives, which meant contributors got no pay and every question was excruciatingly discussed and decided by committee. My cartoons sparked hot debates over the propriety of the word *pussy* and pictures of women treating other women as "sex objects." I was also published in *Wimmen's Comix* and *Gay Comics*. I didn't draw regularly and my work was really pretty bad. At that age, I was too busy living life—that is, chasing girls, going to bars and having fun—and I didn't have the patience to sit still and draw.

Roz: Were you ever tempted to tone down the content of your cartoons so that you wouldn't offend or provoke people?

Jen: I've never drawn anything just to sell. If it doesn't please me, why should I draw it? Of course, this attitude doesn't make me a lot of money, but it's the only way that works for me, and it's much more satisfying.

Roz: One of your postcards was recently found obscene by the post office. How did that come about?

Jen: I got a letter from the U.S. Postal Service telling me that someone had mailed my postcard "Answers" and the post office had seized it. They said it violated the postal laws on mailing "obscene, lewd, lascivious, filthy, vile, or indecent things."

Roz: It's odd that they contacted you—the artist—rather than the woman who had actually sent the card.

Jen: I later contacted the women who sent the card. They said they'd immediately begun mailing more copies of the card with naughty messages written on the back, but none of those were seized. The whole idea is so ridiculous—the cartoon is actually a satire on obscenity. I'd love to fight the case and ask a judge how it can be obscene for a woman to say "Suck my dick." The only thing questionable on the postcard is language. I wish I had the money to pursue this because it would be a fun debate.

Roz: Some of your cartoons provoke an incredibly fierce, angry response from readers. Yet I've spoken with lots of people who've just fallen in love with those same cartoons.

Jen: Reactions to my cartoons are varied. People who disagree with my comics do write angry letters to the publications that print my work.

Roz: When "Communion Wafer" was published in *The Washington Blade*, I was surprised at all the irate letters it provoked. I guess I'd assumed that their readership was a little more open-minded.

Jen: "Communion Wafer" brought the suggestion that I find Jesus. Another cartoon poking fun at gay men brought the suggestion that my cartoons weren't fit to line a cat litter box. People who like the cartoons don't write as often…or maybe I don't have as many friends as I do enemies!

Roz: A lot of editors have told me that readers write in mostly when they get pissed off; it's rare for them to write in to express the fact that they like something.

Jen: The positive feedback is sometimes indirect, like seeing one of my cartoons hanging on a stranger's refrigerator or office wall. And then, there are the wackos—guys who call up wanting to be abused. Some men see my comics and think I'm a dominatrix—I usually just tell them they can't afford me.

Roz: Do you think that people take comics too seriously? Or maybe not seriously enough?

Jen: Well, *some* people take comics too seriously—I'm not fond of the "smellywhiteboy" contingent that permeates comic book stores and conventions, obsessing about comics and keeping them in those plastic bags. Makes me want to get a copy of Superman #1 and rip the cover off. But generally, people don't take a cartoon seriously unless it wins a Pulitzer Prize or makes millions of dollars off licensing fees.

Roz: Why do you think that is?

Jen: Part of the problem is that people don't know how to label cartoonists—we're a mix of writer, artist, journalist, comedian, director and poet. And cartoons come in a lot of formats—newspaper strips, comic books, single panel, editorial, animation and graphic novels. The good part about working in such a misunderstood medium is that it gives the artist a lot of creative freedom; the bad part is that we usually don't get paid much, or get much respect from editors and publishers.

I've supported myself by working in the printing industry doing pre-press production work. I've worked in printing shops, newspapers, and advertising. It's a good field for a cartoonist because I've learned every aspect of the printing industry and I get access to a lot of equipment. Also, it was traditionally a male job, so it paid well, and blue-collar trades are a comfortable place for dykes—you can be yourself and you never have to wear a dress. I've usually worked second or lobster shift, which gives me my days for cartooning, and there's less bullshit from management when you work nights. I've often been in jobs where I'm the only woman with a bunch of straight guys—and it's given me great material for cartoons. Sometimes I have problems with guys who can't handle working with me, but generally after the initial "education" period, I'm

An interview with Jennifer Camper

treated like one of the boys and we talk about cars and girls, and it's pretty comfortable. Things have really changed in the last ten years—there are more women in the field, but the unions have been busted and the old camera work is being replaced by computer.

Roz: Tell me something about the mechanics of how you go about working—what kind of materials you use and how long it takes to do a cartoon, and stuff like that.

Jen: I'm more comfortable and secure with my writing than with my drawing, so I have notebooks of ideas in words, not pictures. Sometimes I just pull out an idea and draw it; other times, I do a cartoon on a specific subject either because it's timely or for assignment. When I was drawing the self-syndicated strip, I'd put out one cartoon every two weeks and a rhythm would develop. I like to have at least five hours of uninterrupted time, but the reality is that I'd usually work like a madwoman on weekends and grab bits of time during the week. I first write the cartoon, breaking it into panels, and then design the layout of the page. Next, I pencil the cartoon; I use a No. 2 pencil on two-ply bristol. After that, I ink it with a technical pen and brush. I draw twice up so that when the cartoon is reduced to final size the image tightens up. My style is very clean and high contrast black-and-white. This look developed partly because I like it, and partly because it reproduces well on the cheap paper of the publications that print my work.

Roz: This past year you've been working on the screenplay for *Nightwood Bar*, the movie based on Katherine Forrest's terrific detective novel *Murder at the Nightwood Bar*. How did you get involved in that project? Has it been fun?

Jen: The director, Tim Hunter, hired me to work on the script. Mary Robison is also one of the screenwriters. It was tremendous fun. Writing for film is a lot like writing comics—the script is only a blueprint and not the end in itself. With both styles of writing, the emphasis is on dialogue, timing and the visual outcome. But with film, no one person has control; everybody is part of an assembly line. Ensemble work can be both terribly rewarding and terribly frustrating.

Roz: Are you happy with the way the script has turned out so far?

Jen: I'm excited about this script because it's a different kind of lesbian film—a murder mystery. Usually lesbian films focus only on a coming out story or a love story and don't show much of a larger lesbian community. When writing gay characters for a mainstream audience, we're often afraid to give a bad impression, and the characters end up flat. *Nightwood Bar* has a whole slew of lesbians, so one single character doesn't have to define all gay women. I just hope if the film gets made, it doesn't get too watered down.

Roz: After ten years of cartooning, how would you say your work has evolved?

Jen: My drawing skills have gotten better, cleaner and more confident. I've gotten some things out of my system and now want to explore more complicated ideas. I'm growing less interested in drawing and more interested in writing. Drawing is difficult because I'm frustrated by the limitations of my abilities. Working on the screenplay of *Nightwood Bar* has got me thinking more about film, too. I've got a lot of projects cooking—we'll see what happens. But I'll still be working with words and pictures whatever form they take.

Roz: Any concluding thoughts about humor?

Jen: Humor is, for me, an attitude. It comes from being a skeptic, questioning the status quo, asking "what if" and "why not?" Something is funny when it's unexpected, a twist on reality that shows you a new way to look at the world. Humor can be used as protection, too. When some guy gives you a hard time on the street, all it takes is some joke about him to give you back your power. And if you can get his buddies laughing at him, too, then this guy will never fuck with you again. People are terrified of being laughed at. And it's not as messy as shooting people. In a cartoon, this translates to satire. The flip side of it is laughing at yourself; this gives you permission to make mistakes. In a cartoon, this translates to the smile of recognition and the relief that someone else does that silly thing, too. People love to laugh. When they're being entertained, they're open to all kinds of ideas they might not otherwise consider.

RONA CHADWICK

"Broadcards"

Perth, West Australia

Rona Chadwick writes: "I am a freelance, feminist cartoonist who, in my other life, arranges training for people who work with young people. For over five years, I have produced a range of wimmin-targeted cards called 'Broadcards.'

"I live in Perth, Western Australia with Sophie, a divinely exuberant Jill Russell Corgi Cross, and Elaine, a mad, Scottish psych nurse. Don't ask me where I get my inspiration!"

In October 1993, Chadwick won two Hysterical Women: First Australian Feminist Cartoon Awards.

Periodicals: *New Woman Magazine, Witty World.*

Collections: *Weenie-toons, Silverleaf's Choice, Fresh Start: Escaping Abusive Relationships, Hysterical Women: A Collection of 100 Australian Feminist Cartoons.*

Also Available: "Broadcards" postcards, Cath Tate postcards.

Formative Influences: Those bleeding feminists!

What I Do to Procrastinate: Read cartoon books and call it "research."

Favorite Music: Women's.

Leisure Activities: Bushwalking with my dog and whoever.

THERAPISTS TO WATCH OUT FOR

KATHLEEN DEBOLD

Beltsville, Maryland

Kathleen DeBold was born into "the obligatory dysfunctional family" in 1950s Brooklyn. In her various manifestations, she has been a fiery activist for women's rights, a Girl Scout Leader, the first female apiary inspector in the state of Maryland, a Peace Corps volunteer, an agricultural development specialist in the Central African Republic, a book reviewer and a towel-folder at a yuppie health spa.

A long-time crossword fanatic, she noticed that gay and lesbian culture was totally ignored in mainstream puzzles, and the few lesbians and gay men included in these puzzles were stripped of their homosexual identity. When a crossword clue was "Baldwin," for example, the answer was always "Alec" or "Billy," never "James" (gay author of *Giovanni's Room*) or "Tammy" (lesbian state representative in Wisconsin). "Stein" was usually a "beer mug," rarely "Gertrude," and never "Lover of Toklas." To counteract this bias, DeBold created the popular Word Gaymes puzzles, which run in publications like *The Washington Blade*, *Lambda Book Report*, the *Lavender Network*.

DeBold is the Deputy Director of the Gay and Lesbian Victory Fund in Washington, D.C. and many of her cartoons are political in nature. She wanted to be included in this book "as an inspiring example of 'If she can do it, anyone can.'"

Book: *Word Gaymes: 101 Puzzles with Lesbian and Gay Themes*, *Out for Office: Campaigning in the Gay Nineties* (editor).

Periodicals: *Sinister Wisdom*, *Common Lives/Lesbian Lives*, *Lesbian Contradiction*, *Lambda Book Report*, *Lesbian Cartoonists Network*, *Sorority*.

Collections: *The Best Contemporary Women's Humor*, *Women's Glibber*, *A Queer Sense of Humor*.

Born: Brooklyn.

Dislikes: Got a year???? The Radical Right, Lesbian Chic, anything chic, group-think, attitude, people who see something bad happening and don't do anything about it, editors who don't return your self-addressed, stamped envelopes, talking or writing about myself.

Most Recent Accomplishment: Edited *Out for Office: Campaigning In the Gay Nineties*, the first book to address the unique challenges of running for office as an openly gay/lesbian candidate.

Leisure Activities: Nagging my lover to work on her next novel, creating crossword puzzles and acrostics, volunteering at a sanctuary for pot-bellied pigs.

RHONDA DICKSION

"Lesbian Survival Hints"
Seattle, Washington

Rhonda Dicksion first came up with "Survival Hints" after hearing that *Lesbian Contradiction* sought cartoons for a special humor issue: "I didn't have anything else to do that Sunday afternoon, so I started thinking about how being a lesbian means you have to hide yourself in public in straight society." With the success of her series, cartooning has become a way of life for Dicksion. "I know cartooning must seem tough to most people—sitting on the porch in the sun thinking, spending late nights at nightclubs researching, endlessly watching videos while inking—but I feel in some way that these small sacrifices are worth the effort.

"I do most of my cartoons, as I am writing this now, in an old overstuffed blue swivel chair that I inherited long ago from some musty relationship. Like most things that are worth having, this chair is plain, familiar and comfortable. I like to think my cartoons are like that (except the plain part, of course)."

Books: *The Lesbian Survival Manual, Stay Tooned.*

Periodicals: *Island Lifestyle* (Hawaii), *Lesbian & Gay News Telegraph, OutFront* (Denver), *Deneuve, Seattle Gay News, Gay Comics.*

Collections: *The Erotic Naiad, The Mysterious Naiad, The Romantic Naiad, Kitty Libber, Mothers!, What Is This Thing Called Sex?, Cats and Their Dykes.*

Birthplace: Los Angeles.

Formative Influences: Cartoons on television (Mighty Mouse, Bugs Bunny, etc.) and comic books (how I learned to read!)

Dislikes: People who turn left in front of me, bicycles on the road, coconut, Rush Limbaugh.

LESBIAN SURVIVAL HINT #140:
NOT ALL COUPLES ENJOY EXPERIMENTATION IN BED.

LESBIAN SURVIVAL HINT #155:
NEVER TEMPT THE FATES.

DIANE DIMASSA

"Hothead Paisan: Homicidal Lesbian Terrorist"

San Francisco, California

If you gave Thelma or Louise the consciousness of Andrea Dworkin, the firepower of Rambo, the build of Martina, and the charm of Pippy Longstocking, then raised her in an Italian Catholic neighborhood, oh, let's say, next door to Madonna, and then you left her in the oven a tad too long, you might have the recipe for Hothead Paisan. —Nancy Boutilier

Like any great work of art, Hothead feels different each time you read her. The first reading, you probably mostly get this powerful catharsis from watching Hothead chop off rapists' dongs. Second reading, maybe you're a little disturbed: isn't Hothead just adding to the violence she opposes? Third reading, you perk up to DiMassa's reminder that Hothead is a satire. You decide not to feel guilty about how much you relish the scene where Hothead flushes a guy's wing-wang down a garbage disposal. Fourth reading, maybe you sort of fall in love with the grenade-toting, cat-smooching blockhead. She's not the Zen ideal, but you forgive her. You tune into all the groovy loveness between DiMassa and Hothead and Chicken (Hothead's cat) and all of Hothead's friends. Fifth reading, you step back from the story and notice how strong and smart DiMassa's art is, and how much better it gets as the issue progresses. You appreciate the nuances in the character's expressions and postures. You wish you could draw like her. Sixth reading, it hits you: this is the funniest stuff you've ever read. You notice details: tampons available in sizes "Normul-flo," "Over-flo" and "Bronto-flo"; panels connected by band-aids. You laugh so hard you almost pee and you are glad, so glad, to share the universe with Hothead Paisan.
—Robin Bernstein, *The Washington Blade*

Book: *Hothead Paisan: Homicidal Lesbian Terrorist.*

Periodicals: *Hothead Paisan: Homicidal Lesbian Terrorist,* the 'zine (#1–16), *Strange-Looking Exile, The Advocate, Frighten the Horses.*

Collections: *What is This Thing Called Sex?, The Best Contemporary Women's Humor, Kitty Libber* (cover art and interior cartoons), *Weenie-toons.*

Also: Coffee mugs, t-shirts, postcards, rubber stamps, acrylic paintings and "No Guilt!" tattoos.

Birthplace: New Haven, Connecticut.

Formative Influences: MAD, *The Winchell Mahoney Show,* Salvador Dali, my kindergarten teacher, Miss Baron.

Dislikes: I hate people who talk too much and don't stop to listen. And vacuum cleaner air.

Leisure Activities: Walking around San Francisco and not knowing what day it is.

Goals: I want to become an incredible painter. Or something....

This is the first appearance of Hothead.

DIANE DiMASSA

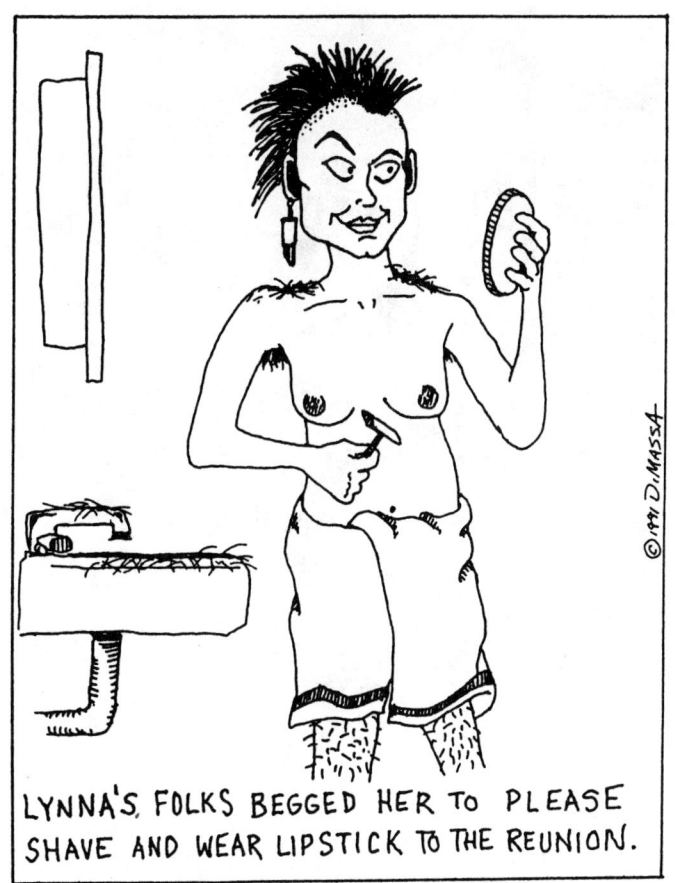

An excerpt from Hothead's response to the bloody debate over the "question" of who controls abortion.

DIANE DiMASSA   54

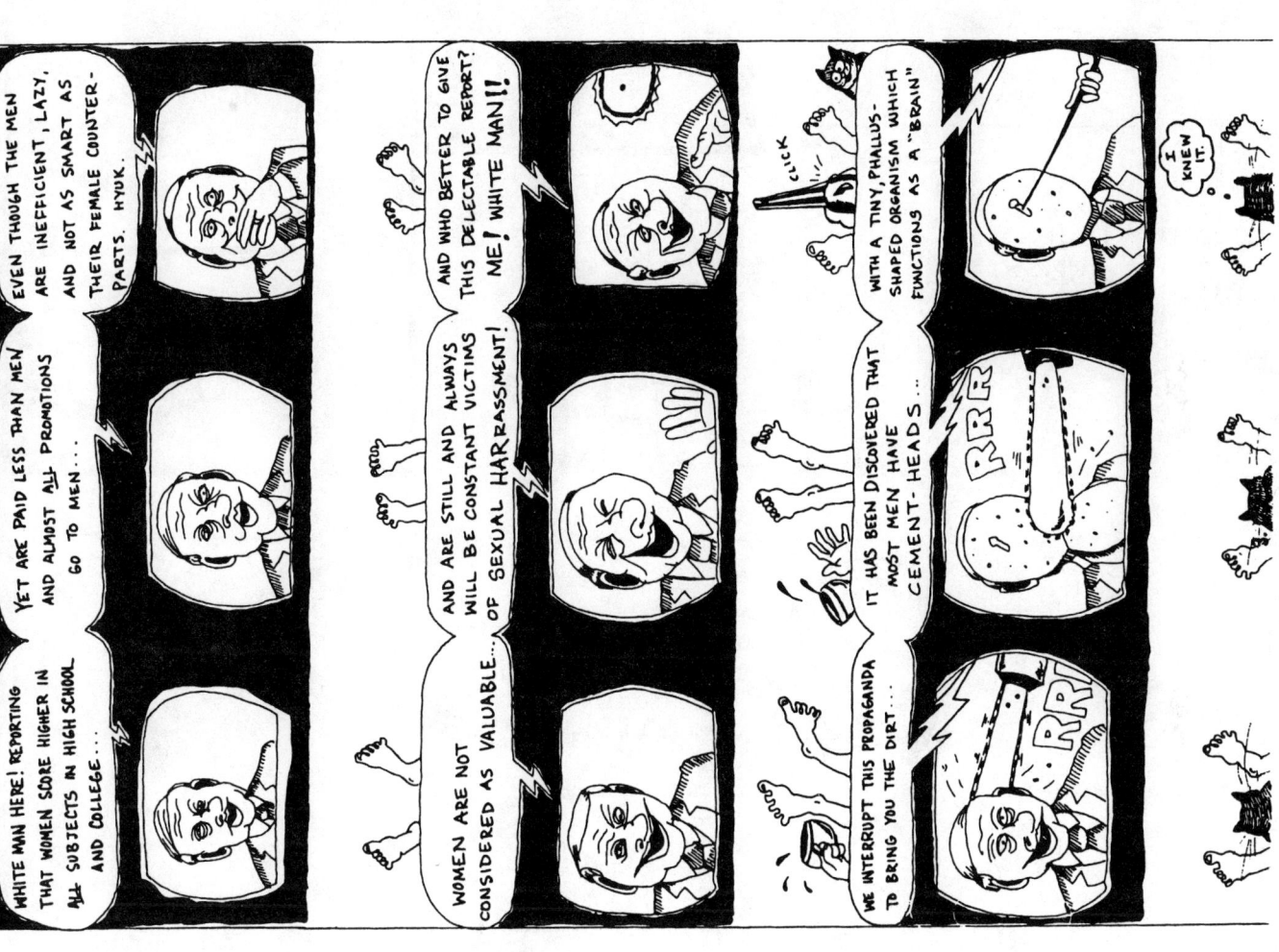

A Rare On-Screen Cross-Section of the "Dick Head"

Diane DiMassa

The robotic medical mechanics of our country, happily cutting and mutilating their way to wealth.

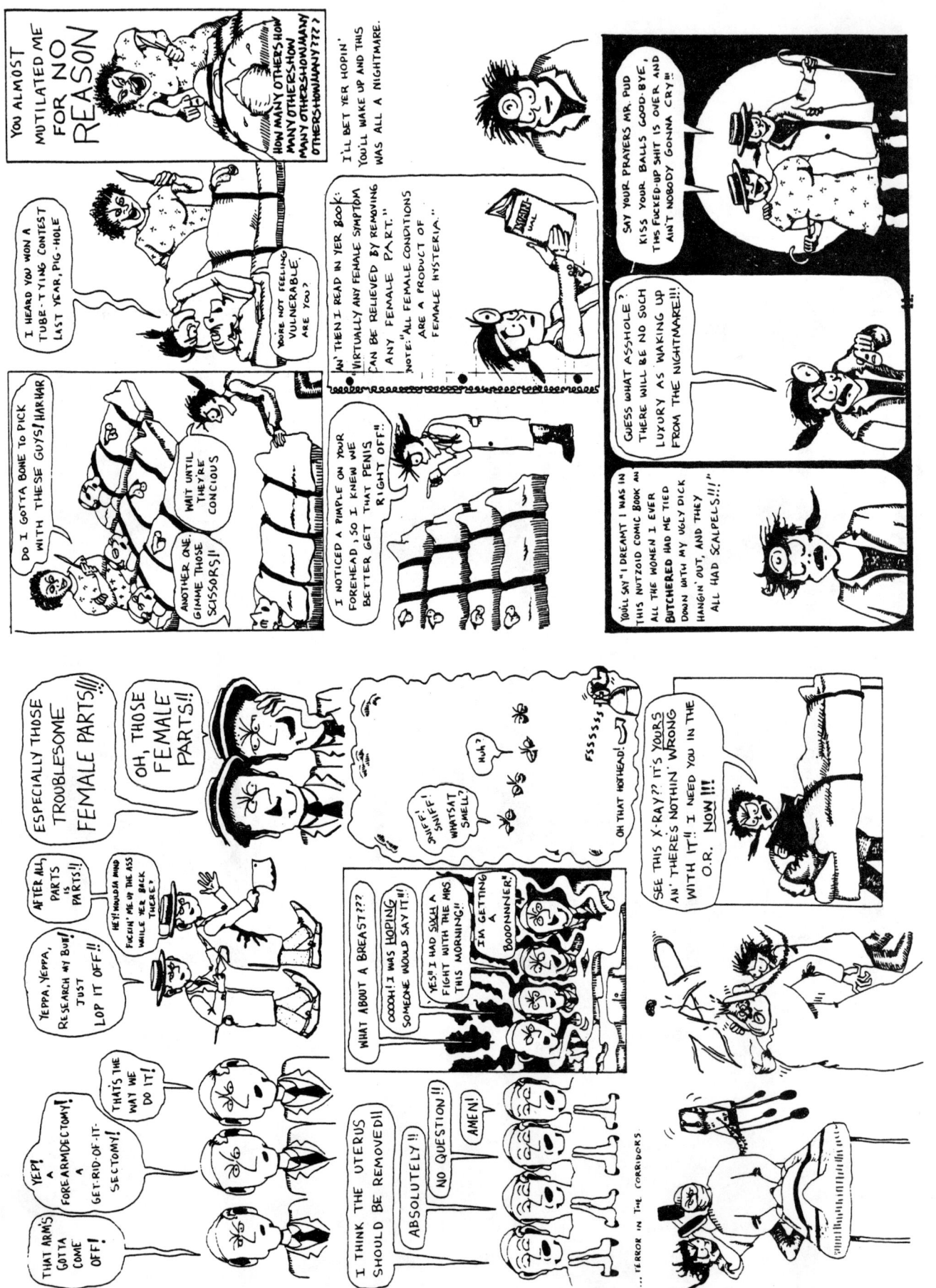

DIANE DiMASSA

Back cover of Strange-Looking Exile #4 "Spill Your Guts" issue.

DIANE DiMASSA

Rape victim as perpetrator; trial as three-ring circus.

DIANE DiMASSA

AN INTERVIEW WITH DIANE DIMASSA

by Elana Bouvier
for *Amazon Country*, a Philadelphia-area radio show

Elana Bouvier: I'm quite pleased to be here tonight speaking with Diane DiMassa, the creator of *Hothead Paisan: Homicidal Lesbian Terrorist,* the socially bizarre dyke that's not quite up to political snuff, who eats meat and likes sex toys, has never protested in Washington D.C., is prone to raving, including vicious mood swings, and into ambushing, farting and hanging upside down. Welcome.

Diane DiMassa: Thanks, Elana.

Elana: Nice to meet you. Those are your words. I don't think I could've put that all together.

Diane: They are.

Elana: Should I call you Diane or should I call you Hothead?

Diane: Diane's fine.

Elana: Okay.

Diane: You draw the line.

Elana: No, it should be *you* drawing the line....

Diane: Yes, I do...often.

Elana: Hothead grew out of your journal, right? How did she come to life? Under what circumstances?

Diane: This coming February, I'll have been doing *Hothead* for three years. When I did the original first four pages—which are pages one through four of issue #1—that's what I was doing in my journal at the time. I brought them to work and showed them around and everybody got a laugh out of it. Then, I just threw them in the corner of my room for a long time. I don't know why. I was newly in recovery—about two or three years. And I was also in therapy working on all this anger. That's really why I did those pages.

Elana: Recovery from what?

Diane: Drugs and alcohol.

Elana: Ah, *that's* nice....

Diane: Excessively. Fifteen years worth of hitting bottom. So I was pregnant with Hothead for about fifteen years and in labor for two before I had her. It was really terrifying to draw at that time because a huge creative block had built up over all those years.

My partner, Stacey, discovered the drawings in the corner of my room, and she had a vision and thought I should try to complete a comic book. She thought there'd be an audience for it. She called around and got prices, and she started publishing *Hothead* as a quarterly comic 'zine. That's really how it started: not with any intention of really following it through to the point where it is now. It was just a project to work on together.

Elana: Did you find it healing when you were starting it or was it too scary?

Diane: It was both. Drawing the stuff and being able to look at it helped me a lot. It's a lot scarier when it's inside. Stuff's always scarier when it's in your head. Or it is to me, anyway. Nothing's scarier than your own imagination. A lot of the stuff that I draw isn't easy to look at. She's very violent sometimes. I don't get a kick out of that. I really have to force it sometimes, but every time I do it, it gets rid of a little bit of it for me. There's something about seeing it where you can look at it, getting it outside of yourself, that gives you a much better perspective.

Elana: Hmmmm.

Diane: Hmmmm. Deeper than you thought, huh?

Elana: I know how it is to show somebody something that you did that comes from the heart or from the soul or from fear. You want them to like it, maybe, or at least respect it.

Diane: Or not burn your house down for it, at the very least.... [*Laughter*]

Elana: Have you been threatened?

Diane: No. Because *Hothead* is published in the form of a comic 'zine and mainly distributed to gay and alternative stores—more underground sorts of venues—so far, it's gotten into the hands of people who are like-minded. Now that it's a book, we'll see. It's going to be in mainstream stores a lot more, and we're anxious to see what kind of crossover attention it gets.

We get a lot of letters from straight people already. Hothead is less about anything particularly lesbian, and more about a slant on how unbalanced society is. So it's more a matter of astuteness among my fans than really gayness...although ninety percent of them are gay.

Elana: Hothead is a major feminist, a real radical feminist, if anything. If I could carry a gun and kill people, it might be fun, too. I might like it. [*Laughter*] Then I'd go home to my little cat, Chicken, and Chicken would help me out.

Diane: Chicken rules!

Elana: Yeah, Chicken rules! Where does this stuff come from? All this anger and all this fear? Is it from the fifteen years of your hitting bottom, or....

Diane: Yeah, and who knows where it started. From when I was a kid, you know, obviously there's been some dysfunction there. [*Laughter*]

Elana: [*In mock therapist voice*] Yes, what was your childhood like, Diane? [*Laughter*]

Diane: Mostly, I just allude to that. The communication in my house was very loud. Whoever could yell the loudest won, and so nobody ever heard what anybody else was saying. So you get out in the real world and you're trying to be an adult and that's all you know how to do, and that doesn't cut it. It's kind of natural that you'd start drinking a lot. As a child, I was very dramatic and probably a little different, and that usually doesn't get encouraged in a kid. Maybe it does more nowadays, but it wasn't with me. So probably that suppression made me really angry, and then it just snowballed. It's hard to know what got heaped onto that pile over the years. A lot. Then, when I got old enough to have all this social consciousness, I was always very aware of who I was and never bought any of the media stereotypes of what women were supposed to be. Seeing all that media stuff, I realized that I was basically invisible to society. And that they wanted me to disappear. So there was no place for me to express myself. So everything just got internalized.

Elana: So doing *Hothead* has been great for you. I've gotten a kick out of reading it. I keep finding myself thinking: "Wow—I've thought about that." I love the section about finding "the right one."

Diane: Classic.

Elana: Very classic. You know—"Does it hold money? Does it have any power, any magical powers?" [*To listeners*] And we all know that we're talking about that male thing, right?

Diane: Men actually say that and have no idea what a cliché and a joke it is. They actually keep coming up with this time after time.

Elana: So how many of your characters are parts of your psyche and your own psychological state?

Diane: They probably all are, you know? The only one who's not really based on someone that I actually know is Roz.

She is the spiritual side of the coin. She's older, and she and Hothead are really good friends for some reason, although they seem really unlikely companions. Roz is blind, and the metaphor there is that the scope of her "vision" is way beyond Hothead's, and her other senses are very developed. She's extremely spiritual, and because of that is able to love Hothead unconditionally and realize that she's on her path and probably doing the best she can, and tries to be as patient with her as possible. And through my getting sober and really having to learn a new way to deal with how I reacted to the world, I've developed a lot of spirituality that I didn't have before.

Elana: Were you an angry drunk?

Diane: Oh yeah, a time bomb.

Elana: Tick, tick, tick?

Diane: Yeah, ten times a day. Extremely angry. Self-destructively. My emotions are really excessive and....

Elana: When's your birthday?

Diane: I have a Scorpio moon.

Elana: [*Laughter*] There we go.

Diane: My feelings were always really, really huge and so I had to get things proportionate to where I was bigger and in control of all this stuff. I just used to be taken by every wind, like a total slave to it. It has not been easy turning it around, let me tell you. Anyway, I've had to develop this Roz-like side which keeps me grounded and anchored and optimistic.

Elana: Do you have a large support system to help you out?

Diane: I went to AA a lot in the beginning. I really don't go too much anymore, because I've integrated the beliefs into my life and live them, rather than sit in meetings. It's different for everyone. I'm not putting AA down or anything. And I also meditate...

Elana: Oh, that's cool.

Diane: ...which is a huge help.

Elana: Is that part of the hanging upside down?

Diane: Yes. Yes. [*Laughter*] And the Zen farting too. And yoga, and so on. Yeah.

Elana: The other character I really like is the dark one that comes out, the other side of the personality.

Diane: Hothead number two?

Elana: Yeah, personality number two. Is that part of you?

Diane: Well, that's me pre-sobriety. That's anger without a conscience. It's just pure anger that doesn't *want* to know any better, that thinks it's okay to go around blowing everything away and blowing everyone away that you don't agree with. That total rage is like a whirlwind that you can't see your way out of.

Elana: Do you think that because this book is going pretty mainstream that people might get the wrong idea? Like a *major* wrong idea?

Diane: They might. This is a classic don't-judge-a-book-by-its-cover situation. The cover shows Hothead stalking down the street with an ax in her hand with this maniacal-looking face and it says "Homicidal Lesbian Terrorist" across the front. I've had women come up to me after my slide show who've said, "I would have never bought this book in a million years if I hadn't just heard your slide show." And they buy it and have me sign it and they love it. Most of the time when I've gotten opposition to *Hothead*, it's from someone who hasn't read it. They see one image and they slam the book shut. Like: "Huh, Castration!" But it is not hard to see the spiritual, tender, pained side of her. You just have to read a little bit of it. And I hope that people do.

Elana: She seems very real to me, and very personable, actually.

Diane: It's hard not to like her once you get into the story because she's really childlike, and she does know somewhere deep down that what she's doing isn't right. But she's so confused by the depth of her own feelings. And the media, too, is a big part of it; she hasn't ingested the media's images of women and white heterosexuality. She never bought into that. But she's taken on the violence that she sees in the media...and of course, she drinks too much caffeine.

Elana: She went to Provincetown. Do you see her traveling the world?

Diane: Provincetown is really the only on-location piece I've done. I wouldn't want to have Hothead go somewhere without actually having been there myself so that I really knew what I was talking about. You'll notice that I really don't get that specific very often. I don't usually use politicians' names and I don't use current events because I don't want the issues to be that dated. I try to keep the focus just on general rage.

Elana: Where do you live?

Diane: New Haven, Connecticut.

Elana: I look at Hothead and I think, "New York City."

Diane: I guess I've modeled it after New York. I spend a lot of time there. Again, I never mention where she is. I leave it open; I want people to imagine it's their town.

WENDY EASTWOOD

Novi Sad, Yugoslavia

Wendy Eastwood writes: "Born in 1964, I was brought up in Gloucestershire, a beautiful county in the heart of the British countryside where lesbians are so invisible that they can't even see themselves! I ran away to study architecture in London, and after my degree I worked for an interior design company for three years, but gave it up because I was more interested in drawing people than the seats they sat in and the buildings where they lived. In 1989, at the request of the editor, I drew my first cartoon for the Christmas issue of Britain's gay and lesbian newspaper, *The Pink Paper*. The strip was so well received that I was asked to continue.

"After living in London for ten years and letting the recession get to me and my day job, I decided to take a vacation in Greece where I met the woman of my dreams who was from former Yugoslavia. Due to various British immigration laws, I threw all caution to the wind and packed my life into my rucksack and now live in Serbia. I am involved in the very small and quiet lesbian and gay movement here and am producing cartoons for their literature. I have been known to appear at demonstrations for peace by The Women in Black and am desperately trying to learn Serbocroat."

Periodicals: *The Pink Paper* (1989-1990).

Collections: *Kitty Libber, What Is This Thing Called Sex?, Ceasefire: Women Against the War, Voyeuse: Women View Sex, HIV & AIDS: Information for Lesbians, Arkadia*.

Drawings should speak for themselves; they are another language, another way of communicating. Cartoons without words give readers the credit for working out what's going on. You can watch an idea growing like a seed and the final frame blooms into Technicolor as the punch line hits you between the eyes.

LESLIE EWING

Oakland, California

Leslie Ewing writes: "I am a middle-aged, middle-class, middle-talented cartoonist whose work has reflected my skewed view of the state of the Lesbian Nation since 1983. I grew up deep behind the 'Orange Curtain' (Orange County, California) as the only child of an only child. I spent most of my childhood with my nose in a comic book or drawing my own stories. For thirty-two years, I tried to be straight to the extent that I allowed myself to remain in a battering relationship with a man for over ten years. During this time, I never drew a thing. In 1980, I finally made peace with myself, came out of the closet, and, as a bonus, rediscovered the cartooning of my childhood.

"My cartoons took on a political edge after my lover and I decided to go to the 1987 March on Washington and participate in the civil disobedience at the Supreme Court. For the next four years, I was very involved with the NAMES Project AIDS Memorial Quilt and acted as the volunteer coordinator for the Washington D.C. display of the entire quilt in 1988 and 1989. During this time, I was lucky enough to connect with a handful of other activists who began a national grassroots organizing effort that resulted in the 1993 March on Washington for Lesbian, Gay and Bi Equal Rights and Liberation. Since the march, I have renewed my concentration on cartooning and currently have an ongoing strip in *Lesbian News* and *Dykespeak*."

Periodicals: *Lesbian News, Dykespeak, Wimmen's Comix, Gay Comics.*

Collections: *Kitty Libber, Strip AIDS USA, Choices.*

Birthplace: Los Angeles.

Creative/Artistic Influences: My mother bought me a comic book every week for probably seven or eight years whenever we went to the market. I was into everything from *Richie Rich* to Rick Griffin's *Murf the Surf*. Later, I was fascinated by the cartoons in *Playboy*, mostly because they were forbidden.

Personal/Political Influences: Getting arrested with my lover in '88 at the F.D.A. was one of the best things I ever did. Activism has taught me that together we are much more than the sum of our parts.

What I Do to Unwind: I'm a gym rat.

Most Recent Accomplishment: Two hundred sit-ups every day...almost every day!

Goals: I stopped thinking of life in terms of goals a *long* time ago.

...Why you will never see me at a Lesbian Sex Club.....

Le Clit Club

HEY LESLIE!!! LESLIE EWING!! WHAT ARE YOU DOING HERE??? I THOUGHT YOU WERE "MARRIED"!!!!

MARRIED!!! DID YOU LIE TO ME?????

HEY... DIDN'T YOU SAY YOUR GIRLFRIEND'S NAME WAS "LESLIE??"

Ohmygod...

HAPPY VALENTINE'S DAY!

Leslie Ewing '94

KAREN FAVREAU

Amherst, Massachusetts

Karen Favreau writes: "I am no longer doing 'gay-specific' cartoons, as I found the genre to be too limiting. My recent involvement and activity in the Libertarian Party has led to cartoons that are much more political and topical in nature, and which lampoon political extremism on both the left and right.

"I am currently living in Amherst, Massachusetts where I'm working as a freelance cartoonist, part-time graphic artist at a health club, art model, and underpaid copy machine operator at Kinko's Copies. Between jobs, I find time to pursue my greatest passion: singing and songwriting. I have begun doing the open mike circuit in Western Massachusetts where I play both solo and with a backup band, doing country cover tunes as well as my own compositions.

Periodicals: *The Valley Comic News* (Northampton, Massachusetts), *The Funny Times, The National Times, Factsheet 5, Metroline*.

Collections: *The Best Contemporary Women's Humor*.

Birthplace: Gardner, Massachusetts.

Influences: I grew up reading MAD, which was my first exposure to satire. I consider it to be the greatest influence on my cartoon style. Currently, I enjoy such "underground" cartoonists as Daniel Clowes (*Eightball*) and Peter Bagge (*Hate*).

Education: B.A., University of Massachusetts, Sociology, 1991.

Heroine: Ayn Rand.

Least Favorite Cartoon: Garfield.

News Topic Which Provided Me with the Most Cartoon Material: Tonya Harding.

NICOLE FERENTZ

"Through Our Eyes"
Chicago, Illinois

Books: *A Lesbian Love Advisor* (illustrator), *The 1989 Working Girl's Datebook: A Calendar for Lesbians, Recovering from Cancer at Home.*

Periodicals: *Lesbian Contradiction, The Advocate, Chicago Reader, Chicago Outlines, Nightlines, Windy City Times, Libido.*

Collections: *The Best Contemporary Women's Humor, Women's Glibber, Mothers, What is This Thing Called Sex?*

Also available: Through Our Eyes, a line of greeting cards for lesbians.

Birthplace: Bloomington, Indiana.

Formative Influences: Etruscan and Medieval art.

Dislikes: Too many to list.

Jobs: Cartoonist, artist, graphic designer, and teacher.

Leisure Activities: Staying home to read mysteries, gardening.

Goals: To come up with a reasonable way to make a living.

FISH

San Francisco, California

Fish writes: "I spent most of my childhood with my face buried in books—science fiction, mythology, fairy tales and adventure stories. For fun, I used to draw Greek and Roman soldiers, dragons and other weird critters. When I came out as a dyke, I realized I didn't know how to draw women at all.

"I didn't start to draw 'seriously' (that is, for public consumption) until I was twenty-two, when I decided that all the fiction I had been trying to write for years took a lot more effort and produced a lot less satisfaction than the doodles I was doing in the margins.

"I was a neophyte in the San Francisco leatherdyke scene at the time, so the subjects that naturally came to mind were sex, leather, and humor—a big dose of humor. Since 1990, I've done lots of artwork for queer sex 'n' politics magazines as well as some comic books and comic anthologies, mostly for free. In 1991, I started a magazine called *Brat Attack: the 'Zine for Leatherdykes and Other Bad Girls* and have published my own artwork in its pages, along with other women's comics and a lot of great writing.

"All the good feedback I've gotten convinced me in the fall of 1993 to enroll in a commercial art school, where I was stunned to discover that there's a whole world out there beyond black writing pens and twenty-pound copy paper. Gosh. Now I'm doing fewer cartoons and more illustration, but not to fear, I'll always keep drawing bad bad girls."

Periodicals: *Brat Attack: The 'Zine for Leatherdykes and Other Bad Girls, Lesbian Contradiction, On Our Backs, Real Girl, Frighten the Horses, Bad Attitude.*

Collections: *What Is This Thing Called Sex?, Women's Glibber, The Bottoming Book: How to Have Terrible Things Done to You by Wonderful People.*

Birthplace: Montreal, Canada—or is that the Independent Republica of Quebec?

Formative Influences: *The Blue Faerie Book*, the Brothers Grimm, Dungeons and Dragons, Asterix and Obelix, and, oh yeah, *The Pearl*—that moth-eaten collection of Victorian pornography that I found in a closet when I was twelve.

Dislikes: Narrow minds.

Leisure Activities: Procrastination, reading, taking my girlfriend's dogs to the beach, worrying about my next project, worrying that I have too much leisure time.

Most Recent Accomplishment: Convincing myself to go back to school for commercial illustration.

Goals: Artistic brilliance, world peace, never having to cook another meal.

One of the very first cartoons I drew, and still one of my favorites.

The characters in "Vanilla Lust" are probably hanging out in San Francisco dungeon parties by now.

"Girls Night Out" is based on a real dream I had. It's the first comic I've ever hesitated to draw, and it took so long to finish that, by the time I got to the last page, I had to go re-do the beginning because my skills had improved so much. I'd say that reading Diane DiMassa's Hothead Paisan made it easier to imagine doing this story, although my characters aren't nearly as cute as little Hothead.

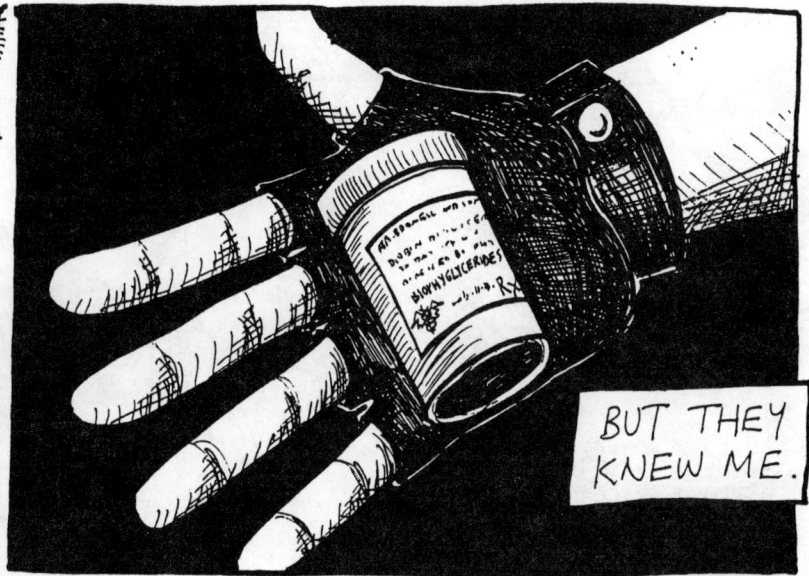

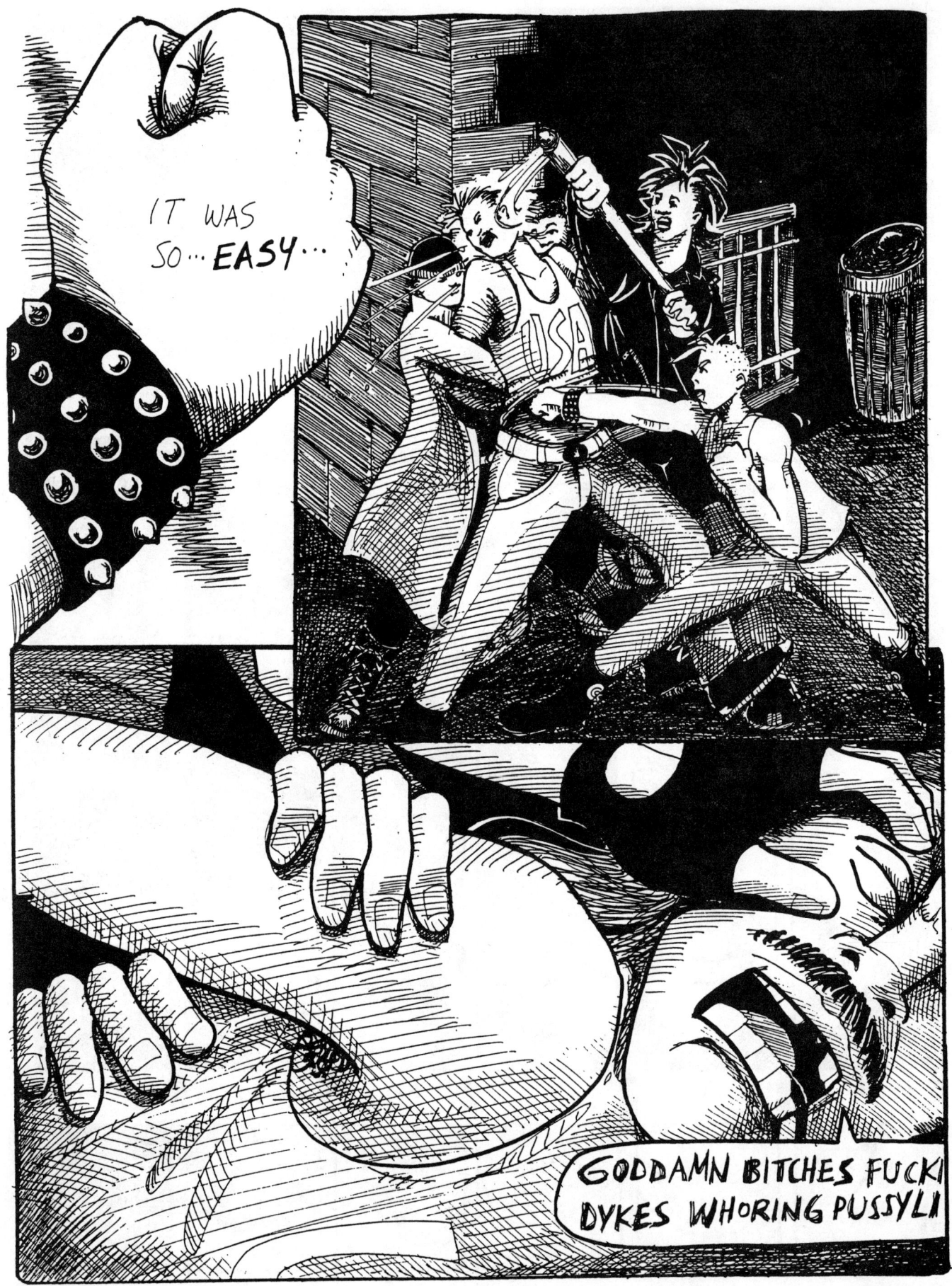

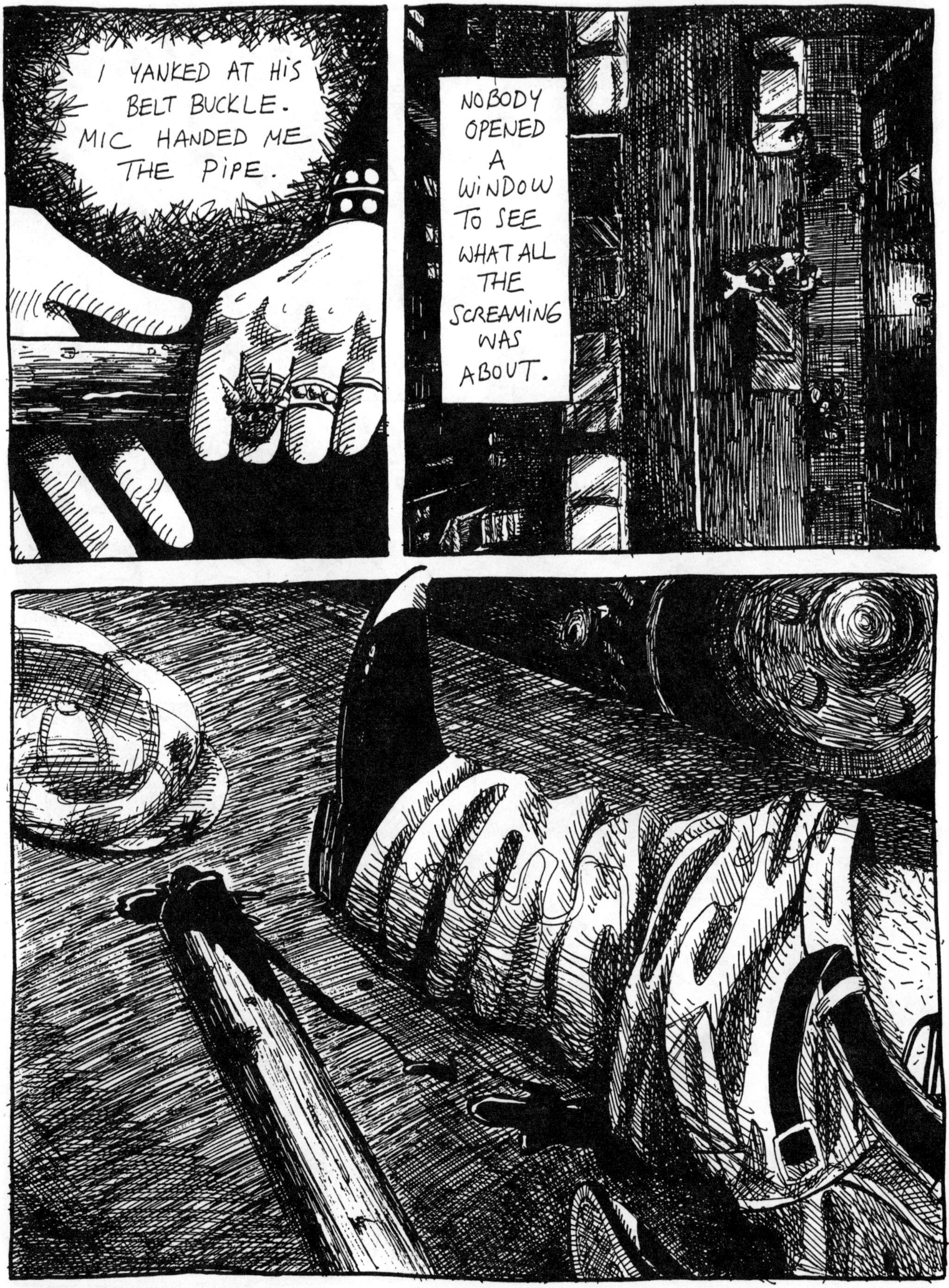

AN INTERVIEW WITH HOTHEAD AND CHICKEN

by Fish

An interview with Hothead and Chicken by Fish

ELLEN FORNEY

"Seven in '75"
Seattle, Washington

Ellen Forney writes: "I am a bisexual vegetarian swimmer, weight lifter, dancer, coffee-drinker, laundry-avoider, phone-gabber, illustrator, comics artist. My mother still has my first recognizable drawing from when I was…I don't know…three years old, maybe. It looks like an ant on a rock, though my mom (presumably, from my own explanation) had carefully labeled it 'Elephant on a Ball.' "

Comic Book: *Tomato*.

Periodicals: *The Rocket*, *The Stranger*, *Bluestocking* (Portland, Oregon), *Ms.*, *On Our Backs*, *Diva*, *Duplex Planet*, *Real Stuff*, *The Village Voice*.

Collections: *The Best Contemporary Women's Humor*, *What Is This Thing Called Sex?*, *Seattle Laughs*.

Also: T-shirts, postcards, posters.

Birthplace: New Jersey.

Formative Influences: Everyone and everything.

Leisure Activities: Swimming, dancing, coffee, talking on the phone with my mom.

Dislikes: Erasers that leave marks.

Day Job: Teaching self-defense.

Recent Accomplishment: My mom and I both swam in Gay Games IV in NYC.

Goal: Wherever the River Takes My Little Canoe.

I came up with the title "Tomato" for my comic because I wanted something that got at the sexual nature of my work. (I didn't set out to do sexually loaded comics, but I guess that's where my interests lie.) I was reading the New York Times and there was a story surveying every "hot potato" of the day. "Hot potato" inspired me to come up with "Tomato," which is perfect because it also means a cute girl.

One of my first and favorite comics. "Birdie" is kind of my alter ego, and this is where she was "born."

From the first issue of Tomato.

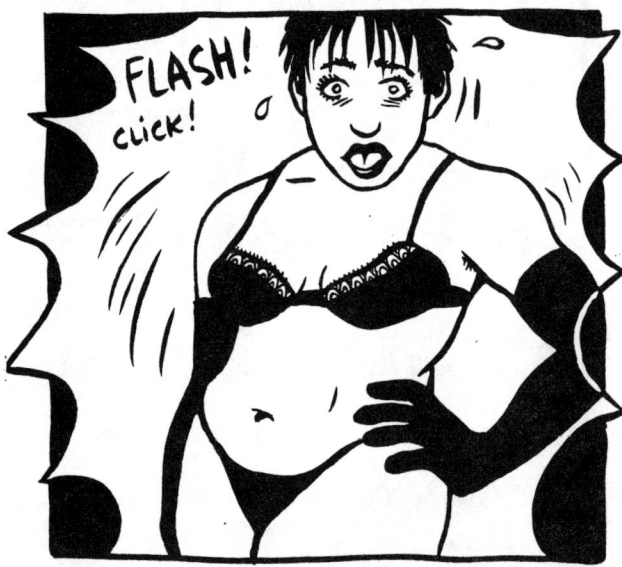

When I first decided to try to do a cartoon for publication, I took a small scribbled thing I'd done for my mom for Mother's Day and turned it into a strip, which took weeks. I sent a copy to Ms. A month or two later, they sent me back a contract. I've realized since then that it was really a fluke for the very first thing I'd ever done to be published by Ms. It was a blessing. And it showed me that it made sense to go for long shots.

I was running once and realized that I was holding my breasts and that it was kind of humorous. I remembered one time, when I was at Michigan, I'd seen a bare-breasted woman running along holding her breasts that way. I'd never seen another woman doing it but knew I did it all the time. Just not in public. I figured that many other women did it too. Since this cartoon has been published, many women have confirmed my suspicions. My male readers are just mystified.

The only thing that isn't true about this story is that I don't have blond hair. But I've always thought about dying it....

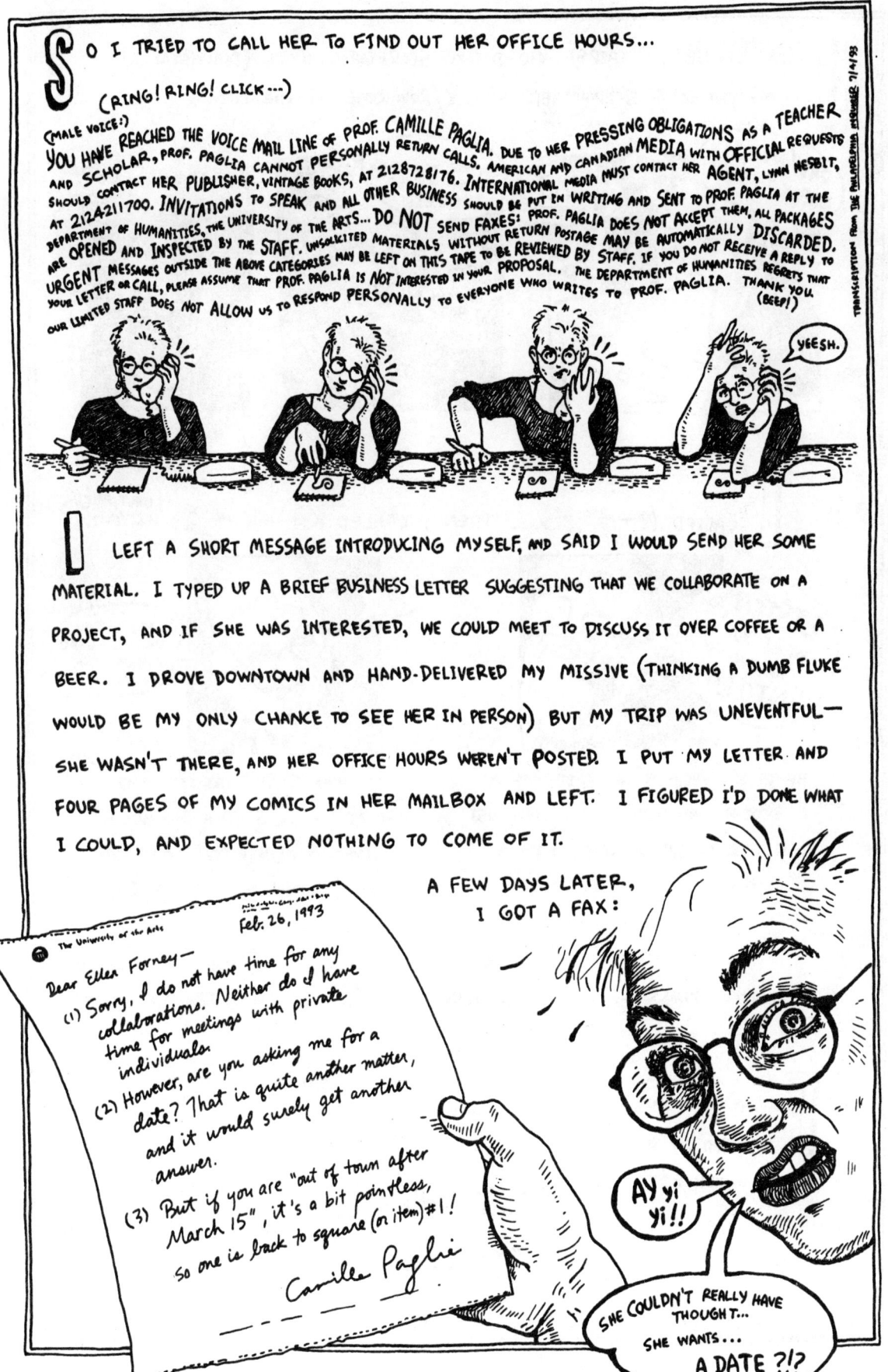

I WAS LIVING (UPSTAIRS) AND DOING SECRETARIAL WORK (DOWNSTAIRS) AT MY FATHER & STEPMOTHER'S OFFICE/ROWHOME AT THE TIME.

I CALLED N——....... THEN I CALLED K—— (ONE OF MY BEST FRIENDS & A PHILA. NATIVE).

HE DIDN'T SEEM TO THINK IT WAS A BIG DEAL. HE THOUGHT I SHOULD JUST ASK HER IF SHE WANTED TO DO A BUSINESS LUNCH.

K—— WAS BESIDE HERSELF. SHE WANTED ME TO SEND A BIG BOUQUET OF FLOWERS WITH A NOTE JUST SAYING WHERE & WHEN AND "SEE YOU THERE" OR SOMETHING, AND SHE WANTED TO SIT AT AN ADJACENT TABLE WITH T——, SO THEY COULD WATCH EVERYTHING. FINALLY SHE SUGGESTED "THE PERFECT PLACE," WHICH I'D NEVER HEARD OF. "OKAY."

FRIDAY AFTERNOON, I DROPPED OFF A NOTE IN HER BOX:

> Friday, February 26, 1993
>
> Camille -
>
> Thanks for your fax this morning. A date? How about Serrano's for dinner tomorrow, say, 7:00? My treat.
>
> Hope to hear from you soon -----
>
> Ellen

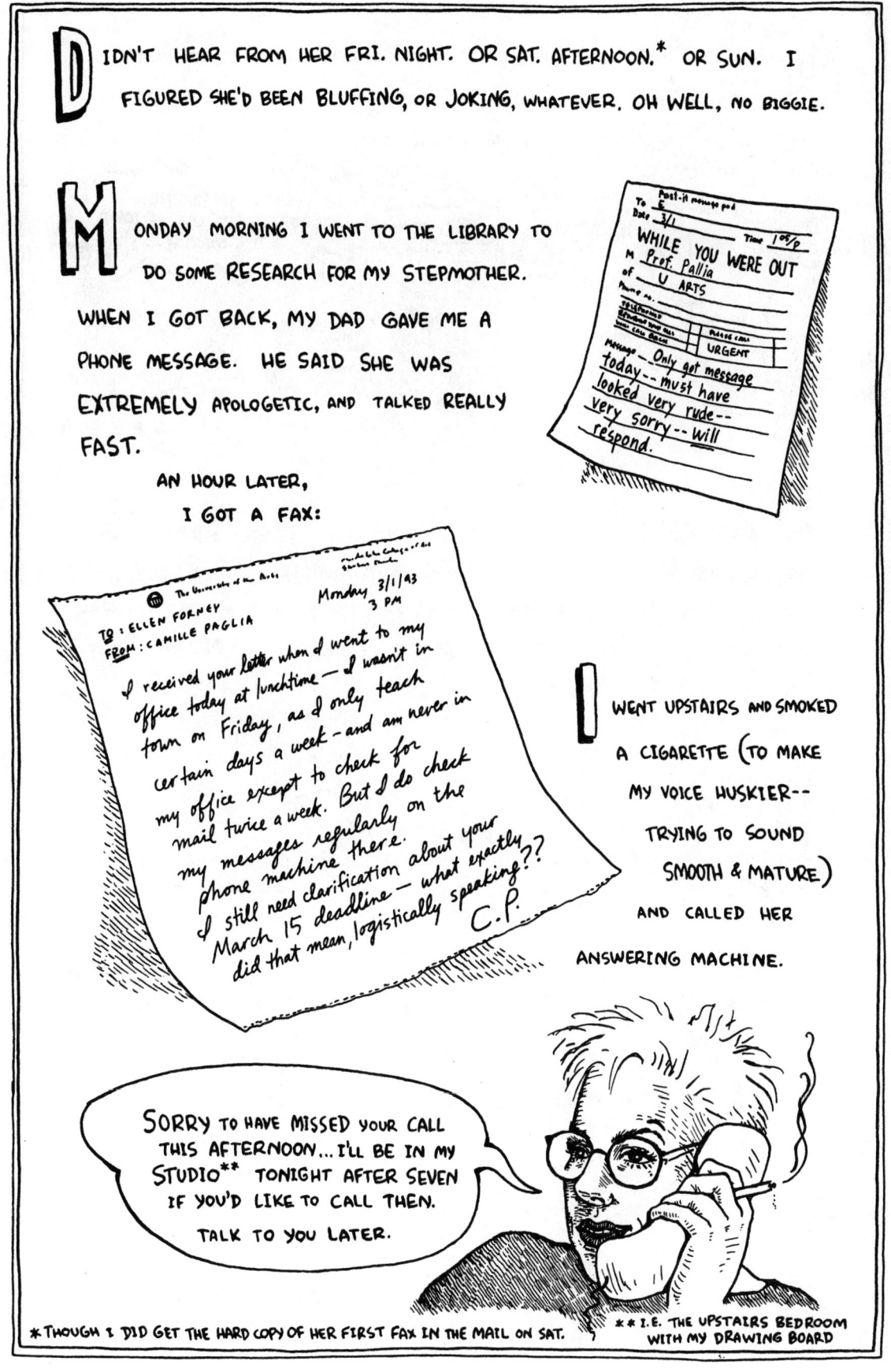

LEANNE FRANSON

"Liliane"

London, England

Leanne Franson writes: "I was born in 1963, in Regina, Saskatchewan, home of the Royal Canadian Mounted Police and the Saskatchewan Legislative Buildings with their bored politicians and drunk-driving adolescents.

"With this inspiring background, I immersed myself in library books, the comics page of the *Leader Post*, and my drawing pad. I admit to having collected only Betty and Veronica comic books.

"In 1982, I moved to Montreal to study Fine Arts at Concordia University. I learned French, expanded my sexuality and stopped drawing (judged too narrative). I continued my education at the Banff School of Fine Arts in 1988 in Ceramics, where my multimedia show 'Indigenous Parsnips' firmly launched me in the direction of topical narrative humor.

"Back in Montreal, I served cappuccinos, did Swedish massage, worked in an art supply store and painted murals (not necessarily in that order), until settling down to a career in children's illustration. In March 1992, when my love life took a turn for the worse, I tried seducing my object of lust, a comics aficionado, with *Liliane* minicomics. I have self-published over twenty issues since then. In 1994, I moved from Montreal to London to check out a possible lifetime love as well as the British comics scene."

Periodicals: *Liliane* minicomics #1–24, *LesboInfo* (Montreal), *Girljock*, *Strange-Looking Exile*, *Brat Attack*, *Dyke's Delight*, *Naughty Bits*, *Equal Time* (Minneapolis), *Gay Comics: Lesbian World* (Euclid, Ohio).

Collections: *What Is This Thing Called Sex?*, *A Queer Sense of Humor*.

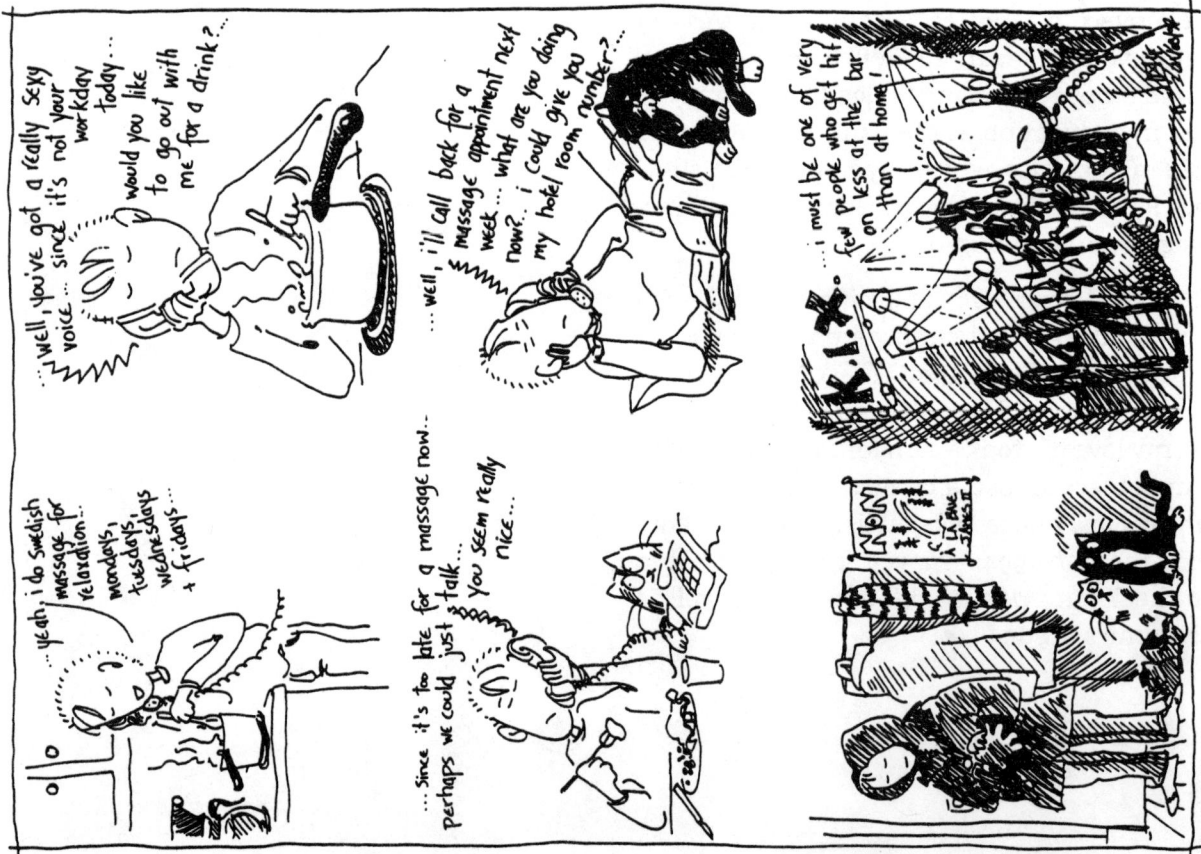

My first minicomic, Liliane: The Fuckin' Faggot, was published in April 1992, signed once again without my last name. I was shown a little photocopied mini by a woman still at Concordia art school and I thought, "I can do that." It's pretty much a true story. I still think it's one of my best, done purely for the fun of seeing if I could do a whole booklet. It was not penciled, and in fact, was completed

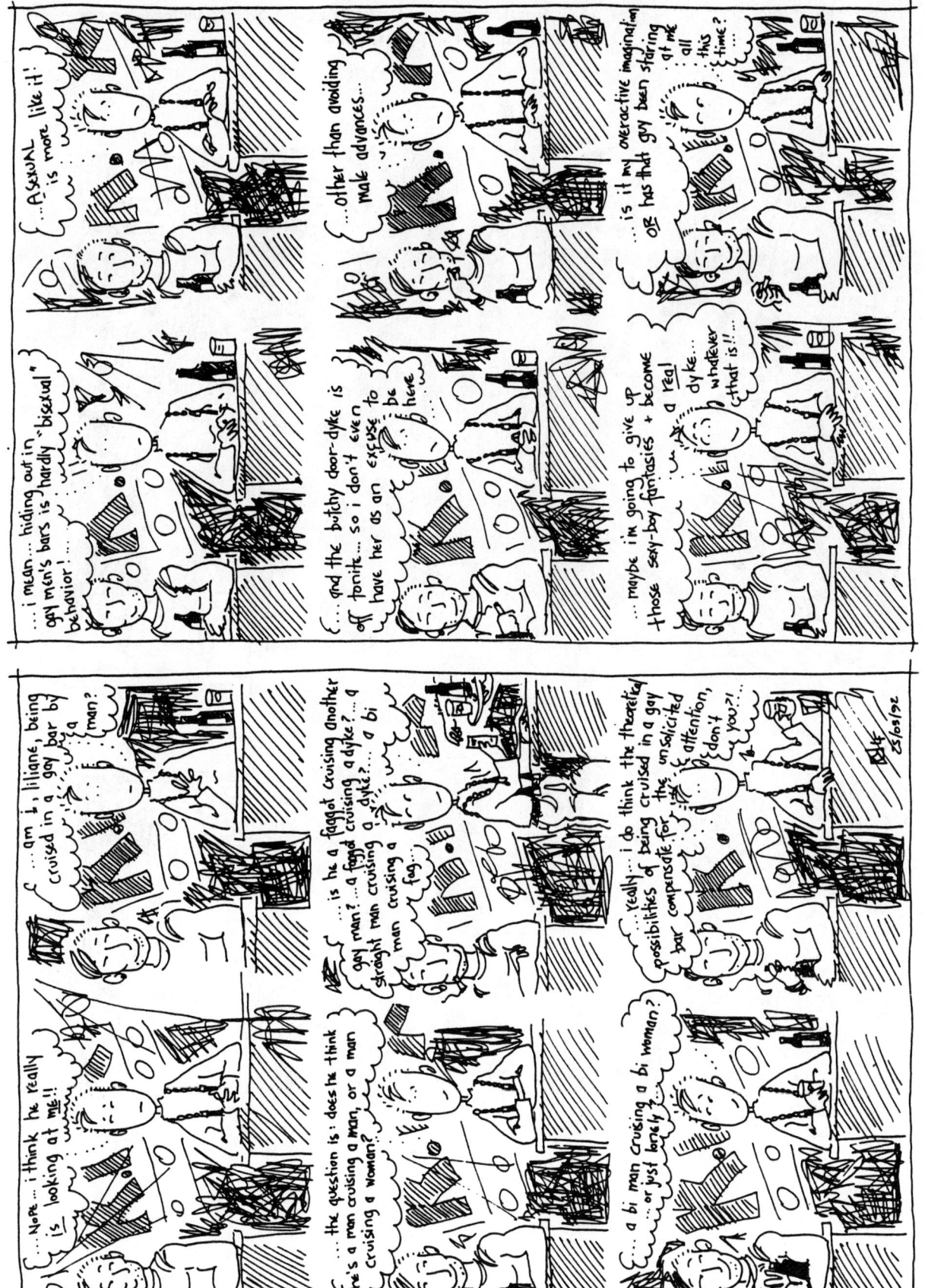

in one evening. I just wish I could recapture that happy lack of self-consciousness. When I got it back, stapled and folded from the copy center, I was so thrilled, I felt I had just been syndicated internationally. The power of self-publishing!

From my comics diary, fall of 1992, an excerpt from a whole series about approaching women in a bar. I like the timing and the self-deprecation.

NIKKI GOSCH

"Baby D.O.T." and "Closet Capers"

Santa Cruz, California

Born May 9, 1965 in Groesbeck, Texas, the first daughter of Roselyn Clutter and Major Larry Gosch, Nikki "spent the best years of my childhood—five years old to nine years old—in Ethiopia. My Dad was an Army officer; we lived on a base in Asmara." The family eventually returned to the U.S., living mostly in Texas, but also in Oklahoma, Maryland, Colorado and Virginia.

"I've known I was a lesbian since age twenty-one," says Gosch, "but I've been a tomboy my entire life." Before she realized she was a lesbian, Gosch wanted to become a nun. "While in Texas, I found a Franciscan order which I truly adored. They took me under their very feminist wings. On the verge of whole-heartedly beginning the official steps, I went to visit my family at Christmas and broke my ankle. Being away from the convent eventually led to my first lesbian encounter. It took a long time to reconcile my religion and my lesbianism. Many girlfriends later, I found the woman of my dreams; Deirdre and I have been together since 1988."

Today, Nikki Gosch and Deirdre Smith co-edit *The Lesbian Cartoonists Network Newsletter*. They live in Santa Cruz with their two "fur children" Peanut and Bosco. Nikki works as a pediatric intensive care nurse in a county hospital and has been cartooning professionally for five years.

Periodicals: *Lesbian Contradiction, Lana's World, The Journal of Nursing Jocularity, Deneuve, Hotwire, Dyke Review, Hysteria.*

Collections: *Women's Glibber, Kitty Libber, Cats and Their Dykes, Le Donne Ridono.*

Influences: Alison Bechdel, Norman Rockwell, Walt Disney, Charles Addams, Charles Schultz.

Favorite Cartoon Character: Tasmanian Devil.

Favorite Books: *Cartooning the Head and Figure* by Jack Hamm, *Cartoonists and Gagwriters Handbook* by Jack Markow.

Previous Day Jobs: Nurse's aide, security guard, trucker, courier, mural artist, donut fryer, state park aide, freelance illustrator, fish processor on a ship in Alaska.

Leisure Activities: Collecting toy cartoon figures and books about cartooning and cartoonists, riding a 1972 Honda motorcycle (named "Sally Brown" after Charlie Brown's sis.)

Recent Accomplishment: Keeping the Lesbian Cartoonists Network alive (with the help of all its members).

A parody on that ol' 'toon (took quite a few comics to find it). Had a big influence when I was a little tomboy. After changing the main character to a woman—I figured out why I was so attracted to it!

CHARLOTTE COMES OUT TO THE WORLD

ROBERTA GREGORY

"Bitchy Bitch"
Seattle, Washington

Roberta Gregory has been doing her best to revolutionize comics for the past twenty years. She was the first lesbian to contribute to *Wimmen's Comix* (1974), making her the first lesbian to "come out" in the underground comic world. In 1976, she was the first woman to single-handedly self-publish a comic book, the ground-breaking *Dynamite Damsels*, a story of a group of friends and their involvement in the feminist movement (copies of which are *still* available). During the rest of the seventies, she lent a rare dyke sensibility to issues of *Wimmen's Comix*, and the woman-owned *Tits and Clits Comix*. During the eighties, Roberta's work appeared in nearly every issue of *Gay Comics*, as well as two self-published trade paperback comics, *Sheila and the Unicorn* and *Winging It*. In 1990, she began the first issue of her sex comic *Artistic Licentiousness*.

Roberta's current act of subversion is the infamous comic book *Naughty Bits*, starring the character "Bitchy Bitch," who's quickly become a cult anti-heroine. With Bitchy Bitch, writes critic Inga Muscio in *Bluestocking Magazine*, "Gregory has managed to create a prototype of femininity residing on the exact opposite spectrum of consciousness as all the beautiful women the media says we're supposed to be. She grabs one's attention in the exact same (yet completely opposite) way as the cover girls on *Cosmopolitan*, *Penthouse* and *Elle*. Her outspoken, undeniable, totally honest ugliness is absolutely, breathtakingly, stunningly beautiful."

The comic is going strong at fourteen issues; Fantagraphics recently published some of the highlights in the book *A Bitch Is Born*. Gregory has received several comic book industry award nominations for *Naughty Bits*, a rarity for a woman cartoonist in what is still a very male-dominated field. In 1994, she received two Eisner nominations, the only female cartoonist to receive *any*, in over *twenty* categories.

Books: *A Bitch is Born*, *Naughty Bits #1–14*, *Dynamite Damsels*, *Sheila and the Unicorn*, *Winging It*, *Artistic Licentiousness #1–2*.

Periodicals: *Gay Comics*, *Graphic Story Monthly*, *Drawn & Quarterly*, *Real Girl*, *Skunk*, *Anything That Moves*, *Wimmen's Comix*.

Collections: *Women's Glibber*, *What Is This Thing Called Sex?*, *Mothers!*, *Kitty Libber: Cat Cartoons by Women*, *Seattle Laughs*, *Strip AIDS USA*, *Choices*.

Birthplace: Los Angeles.

Creative Influences: Early issues of *Wimmen's Comix* and William Blake.

Personal/Political Influences: Every person who strives for individual integrity in the face of overwhelming pressure to conform.

Leisure Activities: I go wandering through the woods and sit on a rock and watch the seagulls fly and look at the water sparkling and if I can't get out of the house, I practice on my Celtic harp.

Hobbies/Interests: I'm a budding radical environmentalist.

Day Job: Production work for Fantagraphics Books (an "alternative" comic book publisher), color separations, silkscreen posters. But it's dwindling to only a few days a month.

Goal: To convert the piles and piles of frenzied scribbling and scrawling in my sketchbooks into readable comics while I still have breath in my body.

This was the first appearance of the character Bitchy Bitch.

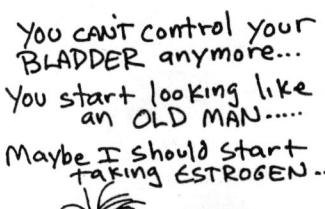

AN INTERVIEW WITH ROBERTA GREGORY

by Robin Bernstein

Robin Bernstein: What do cartoons have to offer queers that other forms of literature don't?

Roberta Gregory: Well, cartoons deal with a wide variety of subject matter, often in a humorous way. It's a very democratic medium. Anyone who can save a little bit of money and have access to anything from a photocopier to a regular printer can be distributed through the same channels as Marvel. I wish more people would appreciate the medium for that point alone. It's probably the medium that's most untainted by corporate interference.

Also, a lot of times, readers can project themselves on the characters and use the characters to see a similar situation from another perspective. It's a very personal, very immediate method of storytelling that has not been exploited to its fullest potential. I think Alison Bechdel pointed out that it's portable and relatively cheap, especially comic books. The average price of a comic book is two dollars and fifty cents, and you can get an hour or so of entertainment from it. You can read it over again; you can read them in sequence once you've got some together. You can loan them to your friends, read them on the bus, on the toilet, in the shower—better than the Internet!

Robin: And you've used comics to address issues of gender and sexuality—particularly in *Naughty Bits*, *Artistic Licentiousness*, *Winging It*, and with "Bitchy Butch."

Roberta: I think comics are a really good format for dealing with gender issues because they're visually oriented. For instance, in *Winging It*, I have a lot of characters who are of dubious gender identity. If it was a movie or a play, the tone of the person's voice would tip off the reader. If it was just prose, I'd have to use pronouns or do something tricky to circumvent pronouns. But if you just have drawings of people and their dialogue, it's up to the reader to decide or project what they know onto the characters.

Robin: You've said Diane DiMassa's Hothead Paisan makes Bitchy Bitch look like a wimp. But I think a much more interesting comparison could be drawn between Hothead and Bitchy Butch. Hothead was created before Bitchy Butch, but after Bitchy Bitch. So, can you talk about connections there?

Roberta: Well, Hothead Paisan and Bitchy Bitch are both asking huge questions with their lives. Both of them seem to be very insecure about the ground they stand on. Hothead reacts by acting out in a way a lot of people would like to do. Bitchy Bitch's turmoil is an inner one. Every now and then, she'll explode, but she doesn't really accomplish anything with it. Basically, it's an outburst of anger that isn't directed, whereas Hothead accomplishes all kinds of mayhem.

I guess, in a way, Bitchy Butch is more rooted in the real world, because her reactions are closer to reactions normal people would have. Hothead has a much more surrealistic story line.

Robin: And Hothead is much more spiritual.

Roberta: Oh, yeah, definitely.

Robin: A lot of your characters have opinions you probably don't endorse. Bitchy Bitch is racist, anti-Semitic, and homophobic; Bitchy Butch hates bisexuals and transgenders. Do you ever worry about giving air time to these opinions?

Roberta: Well, it's not as though people don't think these opinions exist. I think seeing them in context—for example, with Bitchy Bitch, by issue #3, you see where these opinions were formed, you see how racist and anti-Semitic her family is. But I think it's hard for a lot of people to come in cold to certain parts of *Naughty Bits* without getting the whole picture. They just see a few words here and there and don't realize that Bitchy Bitch is not supposed to be a shining example. I guess I'm assuming that the people who read my books are intelligent.

Robin: Here's the lesbian sex question: In *Artistic Licentiousness* #2, the lesbian sex is more explicit than in #1, but it's still not nearly as explicit as the het or gay male sex. Why not?

Roberta: For issue #1, I was assuming there would be a larger male readership than a female readership, and I had this gut reaction; I did not want to show het men what lesbians do. I had this protective kind of feeling, like I'd be betraying every woman I've been in bed with. Guys that want to see "lesbians" having sex so they can masturbate to it have plenty of bad examples of comics drawn by het men who think they know what lesbians do.

That's one of the few times I had a negative gut reaction to doing something, because usually I'm pretty "damn the torpedoes" about being explicit. It felt like something I wouldn't be able to live with afterwards. I hate to disappoint my lesbian readers, but they have plenty of that stuff.

Robin: Well, not plenty of it.

Roberta: That's true.

Robin: So do an all-lesbian smut comic!

Roberta: Okay. I actually did a couple way back, but they never got published.

Robin: You've written a lot about distrust and animosity between bi women and lesbians. What would you like to see?

Roberta: I think we've got everything to gain and nothing to lose from letting everybody's experience speak for itself, rather than questioning someone's credentials. The women's movement has taught us that divisiveness works against us.

The religious right—they don't care about the fine distinctions between whether someone is a Kinsey five versus a Kinsey three, or whether they're biologically male or female. To them, we're all just queers, and they see us as a threat. I think it's really sad that people are letting petty details cause divisiveness, instead of accepting the fact that there's room for everybody.

Robin: You've addressed the religious right in both *Naughty Bits* and "Bitchy Butch." How has the religious right touched your art?

Roberta: The religious right has affected my art because it really bothers me that they're presenting such a narrow view of Christianity. I believe that if people loved one another and forgave each other and followed some of the teachings of Jesus, this world would be a much better place. But the problem with religious righters is that they're perverting what are, at heart, very positive concepts and turning them into tools for their own ends. I think the religious right is probably the biggest threat to the gay community—or any people that represent a minority opinion. The religious right is one of the few topical subjects I deal with in my work because they're particularly active in the Pacific Northwest and Washington State.

Robin: Besides *Naughty Bits* and *Artistic Licentiousness* and your other regular comics, what should we look for next from you?

Roberta: In non-print, there's going to be a Bitchy Bitch doll. And there's the Bitchy Bitch stage production with some people in Seattle. I've also done the pencil work for a two-minute animated cartoon with Bitchy Bitch. That was originally suggested by Colossal Pictures, the people who do the animation for MTV. They tried to sell it to MTV, and it came really close, but I guess someone realized that that was a tampon and that was menstrual blood and it would probably frighten away the Beavis and Butthead viewers.

JOAN HILTY

New York, New York

Joan Hilty writes: "I'm twenty-six. I was born in Kentucky and toilet-trained in Liberia as a Peace Corps brat, but grew up in Larkspur, California, just north of San Francisco, drawing cartoons from a very early age. I majored in art at Brown University, taking classes on the side at the Rhode Island School of Design. In 1989, I moved back to San Francisco where I got support from Trina Robbins and Caryn Leschen, Roxxie, Angela Bocage and Robert Triptow, cartoonists and editors who were happy to publish my weird stuff. I began a regular feature for *The Advocate* in late 1992. I now live in Manhattan and have been developing a feature for daily newspapers, an on-the-road female buddy strip that has won honors in cartoon contests sponsored by *The San Francisco Bay Guardian* and the *Boston Comic News*, and has attracted some interest from syndicates."

Books: *Immola and the Luna Legion*, *Lesbomania* (cover art and illustrations).

Periodicals: *The Advocate*, *Girljock*, *OH...*, *Gay Comics*.

Collections: *Kitty Libber*.

Birthplace: Lexington, Kentucky.

Influences: George Herriman ("Krazy Kat"), Herge ("Tintin"), Jaime Hernandez (*Love and Rockets*), country music, feminism, junk food.

Dislikes: Misogynists-R-Us comix, Newt Gingrich, static electricity.

Leisure Activities: Volleyball, road trips, surfing America Online.

Most Recent Achievement: Doing a solo comic book and learning how to install a phone line without stapling my hand to the wall.

Goal: To be in newspaper comics, to get profiled in *People* magazine, to own ten dogs, and to live a day in the life of Elvis Presley circa 1973, only with less drugs.

In New York, NY, Sophie is aging her hairstylist prematurely.

Seattle, WA...

Luisa whups the field in a masters' singles race and forgets her manners.

At the New Year's parade in San Francisco, CA, Amy is busy cruising Miss Chinatown 1992.

In Austin, TX, Jen is about to make the biggest mistake of her life.

"I'D LIKE TO SEE YOU AGAIN."

Denver, CO: Dani obligingly gives a brief history lesson to a young, attentive queer-basher.

"IN BATTLE WE CHEYENNE WOULD 'COUNT COUP,' MEANING TOUCH A FOE TO SHOW HOW EASILY HE COULD BE KILLED, BUT CHOOSING NOT TO, THEREBY SHAMING HIM. PROVED COURAGE AND SUPERIORITY. DON'T YOU THINK SO?"

And at day's end in New Orleans, LA, Willie is still chafing under her vow of secrecy regarding the two actresses who checked in at eleven.

END

Everyone thinks I made up "Debbie Does Boots" but she really did do boots, at the Nexus/Petticoat bar in Austin.

I got in trouble for this one, but not from anyone in Hollywood. An angry reader wanted to know why I had slammed Slavs by using the Slavic name Zitvo for a conniving, gap-toothed power broker. Actually, it's an anagram for real-life superagent Mike Ovitz, and the character is a caricature of him, right down to the gap. I had no idea Zitvo was a real surname. Now I know.

JOAN HILTY

I figure Monk magazine can't cover it all. Anyway, this one and "Oscar" were done en route to New York on tabletops in Washington and New Mexico.

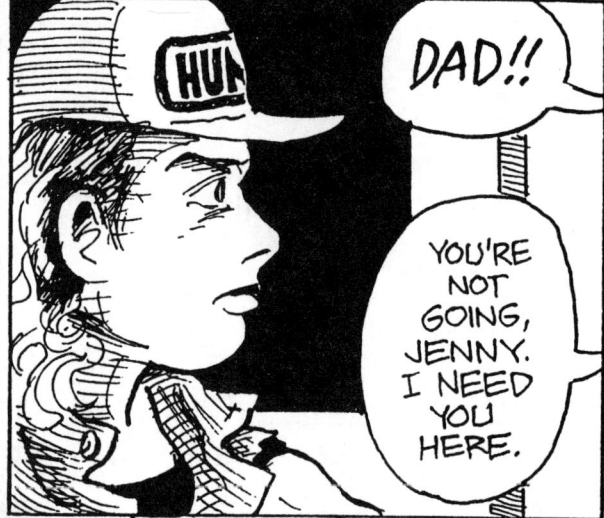

CATH JACKSON

London, England

Born: Aldershot, United Kingdom. To Joyce and Peter, a second daughter.

Early Creative Influences: Jules Feiffer, for making gloom funny.

Later Creative Influences: Jo Nesbitt, and the Sour Cream collective, who put British lesbian feminist humor on the drawing board; Nicole Hollander, for Sylvia, who says it all; Harpur of the *Guardian* newspaper, who refuses to make a fuss about being the only female mainstream political cartoonist working on a national daily paper in the U.K.; Christine Roche, for her powerful drawing; Angela Martin, who manages to be wicked, witty, deadly sharp *and* a radical feminist.

Books: *Wonder Wimbin*, *Visibly Vera*.

Publications: *Trouble & Strife*.

Collections: *Women's Glibber*, *What Is This Thing Called Sex?*

Dislikes: You name it. I've probably hated it.

Leisure Activities: Long country walks, day-dreaming, ambling around art galleries, reading detective novels.

Recent Accomplishments: Getting by.

Goal: To paint big and bold portraits in oils, full full color, with latherings of paint and no black lines or cross-hatching.

ON READING FREUD

PLINK

KRIS KOVICK

San Francisco, California

Kris writes: "I started drawing when I was five or six years old, and was encouraged to draw because it kept me quiet. I could escape into a world of my own creations. My parents called my drawings 'little men.' I didn't have the nerve to correct them, 'That's lesbians.'

"I come from a big artistic family. Everybody draws and plays music and tells lies. My mom is also a cartoonist. She worked for Disney before marriage. Now she is a soft-sculptor. She embroiders feminist slogans onto hot pads and sells them for her charity, the Republican Party. She is the original 'Ladies Against Women' lady, and my grandfather was the notorious sculptor, Vladmir Kovacevich. His mobiles were to Wilsonia what the Watts Towers are to L.A. My work falls somewhere in between theirs."

Books: *What I Love About Lesbian Politics is Arguing With People I Agree With, Glibquips: Funny Words by Funny Women* (cover art and illustrations).

Periodicals: *Deneuve, Frighten the Horses, Girljock, The Washington Blade.*

Collections: *Women's Glibber, What Is This Thing Called Sex?, The Best Contemporary Women's Humor.*

Birthplace: Wilsonia, California.

Birthday: Kris shares her birthday, September 10, with Alison Bechdel and jokes that she's Alison's "evil twin."

Beloved Cartoons and Cartoonists: "Calvin and Hobbes," Alison Bechdel, Senator Snort, Bullwinkle, "Herman," Bugs Bunny, Bambi (I love Disney, but hate Disneyland), I liked "Doonesbury" in the sixties, Oliphant, *New Yorker* 'toons, Tom of Finland, Joan Hilty, Andrea Natalie, Donelan, "Far Side," Animation Festival, Porky Pig, Road Runner, Angela Bocage, *Gay Comics*, love *Hothead Paisan: Homicidal Lesbian Terrorist*, Roz Chast, Julie Dusset, Jennifer Camper, Prof. I. B. Gettendown, Roxxie, Roberta Gregory's Bitchy Bitch. (This is only a beginning.)

Arrests: Many.

Inspiring Quote: "We are all two lovers away from Jodie Foster."

Most Recent Accomplishment: I just finished chemotherapy. Looks like I'll live.

What She's Doing Now: Producing spoken word performance art at Red Dora's Bearded Lady in San Francisco.

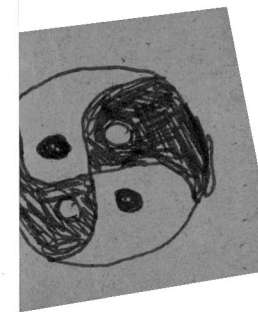

I drew this cartoon when I was very angry about AIDS and the military ban, the Christian Right and the general assault on homosexuals in America.

My folks.

I was asked by Absolut Vodka to draw a cartoon for an ad. Although I was in recovery, I needed the money and I did it. Absolut sent me a kill fee, and declined to use it.

POOR WOMAN'S FACE LIFT

I discovered by pulling my hair back into a severe bun, I could stretch my face out smooth again. I'm vain, but I'm on a budget.

I love San Jose. Nobody's a butch or femme. Everybody's corporate.

Stone Butch Blues by Leslie Feinberg made me re-think my entire wardrobe.

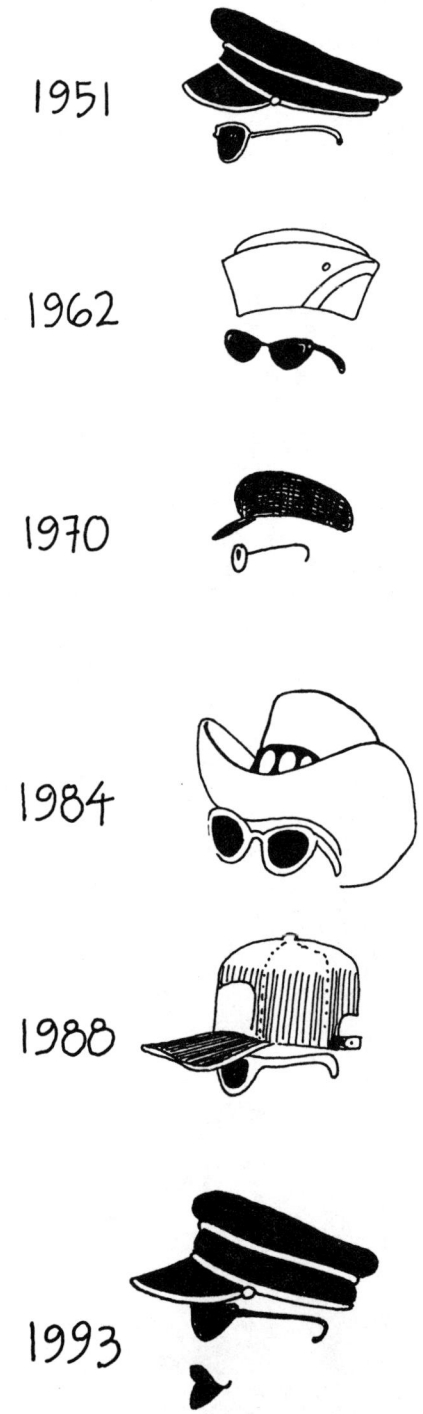

This cartoon is a rip-off of a booze ad. It's supposed to signify that good things out-last fads...but it also illustrates the Marxist dialectic. Whatever. It begins on my birthday, when dykes were scary, and then proceeds through my journey into Tomboy Nation: Fascist Tomboy, Intellectual Tomboy, Good 'Ol Tomboy and Tomboy Geek and finally to the Socially Reconstructed Lesbian of the 1990s, if you will.

I love poodle skirts—what can I say?

I took Alison Bechdel's characters, Mo and Harriet, to the sex club before they broke up. I fell asleep under a chair, so I really missed the action.

HUNGRY DYKE® FROZEN DINNERS

WITH A FOLDED **PLAID NAPKIN** INSIDE EACH PACKAGE

YOU BETTER SEND SECURITY... SOME MILITANT VANILLAS ARE CHALLENGING THE S/M DYKES TO A GAME OF ULTIMATE MOTHER MAY I. ITS GONNA BE TROUBLE!

This is supposed to be the Michigan Womyn's Music Festival. The drawing comes from a photo of Dykes on Bikes right before the gay pride parade starts. Dykes on Bikes leads the parade and it's always fun to try to hitch a ride on the back of a stag dyke biker and ride bitch (or behind). It sounds so dirty now.

AN INTERVIEW WITH KRIS KOVICK

by Emily Greenberg

I first met Kris Kovick several years ago in San Francisco. A friend of mine suggested we relieve our boredom by going for a walk to visit Kris, who was a pal of hers. Kris invited us in, and when we explained that we had dropped by for some entertainment, she sat herself down in a comfortable chair and told us the story of Helen of Troy, complete with gruesome, bloody detail, feminist subtext, and guitar soliloquy. Afterwards, Kris showed us the latest cartoons she was working on. Needless to say, I have been a fan ever since.

To my amusement, Kris began our recent interview by telling me another story from Greek mythology. Actually, she started off by telling me about her latest sexual exploits, to which I politely expressed some doubt....

Kris Kovick: I'm not a liar! I'm a truth-sayer. In fact, I have a Cassandra complex. Do you want to know what a Cassandra complex is?

Emily Greenberg: Sure.

Kris: Cassandra was King Priam's daughter, and Priam was the King of Troy. During the Trojan war, Troy was besieged and Troy was falling. Cassandra was taken as a spoil of war.

Emily: Oh, yum!

Kris: Yeah, right. It was not a cool thing for her. She was really freaked out, and she was picked out by the commander of the Greek army, Agamemnon, as a little bauble—a souvenir. She was beautiful, and she was the king's fucking daughter, and she was going to go live and be his foot stand, right? Well, what happened was that the experience of going from being a king's daughter to a spoil of war made her crazy. And her craziness was a peculiar, interesting kind of craziness. She became lucid. She could foretell the future and she told the future and she just babbled and babbled and babbled....

Emily: And this is where you come in.

Kris: Yeah! I have a Cassandra complex. People think I'm crazy, but I tell the truth. I don't lie and I don't have to lie. The truth is way more interesting than any lies I could tell. I could tell some good lies, but the truth is even better. Lies are Sweet 'n' Low, whereas I got the real sugar.

Who knows? Maybe she is a truth-sayer. Maybe her short story ("Hair Pillow," printed in Frighten the Horses) about her brother coming home to small town Wilsonia for Thanksgiving, wearing a gold lamé suit and showing the aunts and uncles a picture of his beloved fiancée, the one and only Miss Divine, is the truth. It's a damn good story, and I wasn't going to argue with her.

Emily: What are your favorite 'zines these days?

Kris: Well, I like a 'zine called *Holy Titclamps*.

Emily: I've never heard of that one.

Kris: Yeah, it's good. I really like the guy who does it because he talks about appearance and reality, which I think is the most important thing for people who are into the 'zine scene to really think about.

Emily: I'm shocked that you wouldn't pick a lesbian 'zine.

Kris: Well, I don't make too big a distinction between gay and lesbian because of AIDS, you know?

Emily: Huh-um.

Kris: I mean AIDS has reduced, AIDS has changed everything. I think lesbians are probably going to become a favored minority. I see a lot of advertising that shows girl-on-girl live action. What I think that's about is not just lesbians being a favored minority, but a whole marketing strategy using lesbianism.

Emily: What about *Frighten the Horses*? That's not just girl-on-girl, that's girls with knives.

Kris: *Frighten the Horses* is like Thelma and Louise breaking out of the insane asylum and finding automatic weapons, but instead of automatic weapons, they're using verbs and nouns. We're not going to kill people with verbs and nouns, we're going to empower people with ways of saying things and responding to things that are not based on the same old profit motive, not the same old business as usual. That's one of the things I like about *Frighten the Horses* and I like that about *Holy Titclamps* and I like that about *Logomotion* and I like that about the whole 'zine scene, in fact. It's not about business as usual. They do not give a shit about advertising or offending the reader or having a bigger readership. They care about the issues as they see them.

Emily: What do you think about the less offensive new magazines like *Deneuve*?

Kris: *Deneuve* is a magazine that will reap the benefits of what I think is going to happen to lesbian culture. And what I think is going to happen is this: There was an issue of *Image* magazine that dealt with two San Francisco lesbian supervisors, Achtenberg and Migden. All the ads in that issue were girl-on-girl ads.

Emily: And this is a straight magazine.

Kris: This is a straight mag. The back cover was a Chanel ad, and it had two women sitting on a fence, on a picket fence! Well, I mean, that said a lot. Every ad in that magazine had two women in it. And what that said was the image of two women can sell products better than tits and ass can, and that's the truth. Liberated women see two women in an ad, no matter what they're selling, and they say, [*Snap*] "Far out! We have come a long way, baby." Gay men see it and they go, "Oh [*Snap*] sister!" Straight men see it and they transpose themselves onto the advertisement between the two babes, and lesbians see it and say, [*Snap*] "Right on! For once, here we are!" So girl-on-girl advertising, I think, throws a pretty wide net.

Emily: When did you start cartooning?

Kris: I started cartooning when I was a baby. I started drawing when I was three or four.

Emily: Do you have any of your baby pictures?

Kris: No. Maybe my mom does, but my mom really disapproves of my, uh-um, my mom was a cartoonist, did you know that?

Emily: No, I didn't know that.

Kris: Yeah, and my dad was a beautiful wood carver, my sister is an oil painter, my brother—just a bizarre artist. And so, in my family when we had a family discussion, all five of us would be drawing the entire time. Everyone in my family draws....

> *Thanksgiving is our big family holiday because even though it's imperialistic, it's nondenominational, and each person in my family is a different religion. It's like Belfast meets Beirut.*
> —"Hair Pillow"

When I was a kid, when I was about twelve or thirteen, I knew I was going to be a writer. I don't know why. I couldn't even conjugate the simplest English verbs. I wasn't a good student at all. But I knew that I loved to tell stories, and my grandfather was a great storyteller...I went to San Francisco and sort of struck out on my own, and a lot of funny things happened, but I didn't get hurt. And that's where I think short stories come from. You put yourself in an unfamiliar situation and you don't die. I also write short stories because I meet someone who inspires me and I want to send them a bouquet, only a bouquet [*Snap*] is so easy, it's just ten dollars, and instead I'll write them a letter that has some weird story in it, and they feel like "Oh god, this is so sweet, I can almost smell it!" And that's why I write short stories, it's a form of flirting. [*Laughter*] Yeah, I do it for the dates.

> *Her hands were beautiful. The color of her skin was an iridescent brown, like gravy. I worship gravy like a God; it's the religion of white bread.*
> —"No Embarazado"

Emily: Do you think you're turning more into a writer and becoming less focused on cartooning?

Kris: Yeah.

Emily: That's where you're heading?

Kris: Well, I don't want that. What I want to do now is to bring out a book that's more writing and fewer cartoons, but there will be cartoons it, too. I've tried to make the cartoons more complex—the drawings will have more texture, but the drawing will be simpler. I want to make the material, the fabric of people's clothing more interesting, but their poses more simple. And I want less text; I want you to understand what they're saying to each other by their body language. That's where my drawing is going. So I actually like my drawing better, but that kind of drawing takes longer.

ERIKA LOPEZ
★★★★★★★★★★
an AMERICAN ART chick

THE BEGINNING → "I was born in NYC in 1967. My mom conceived me all by herself because she's awesome. And allow me to publicly say that my mom, Deborah Reese, is an amazingly courageous, funny, wise woman + I love her + thank her for her strong love + support. I even feel it 3000 miles away."

FORMATIVE INFLUENCES → "Getting fired a lot; talking to old people; and looking at people's faces when they don't know you're looking."

therapy girl as a little child

"Honey, your mother and I are crossdressers. We're also getting divorced..."

LOPEZ

DISLIKES → "Working for other people and paying them rent. / I don't like it when vegetarians are whiny control freaks and later admit they still eat chicken or prawns. Whatever... I say, relax, open a window... go out and Live. Laugh so hard you start crow's feet. We're all gonna rot one day. → Oh, and I don't like it when people get attitudes like THEY'LL never rot. Like, they think if you dig them up 50 years after they die, they'll still look so good you'll still want to have sex with them. / OH → and I'm tired of people talking about sex in a fake-shocking way. BORING! whatever" ← (whatever to the tenth power)"

MOST RECENT ACCOMPLISHMENTS "Getting published more regularly + building a nice solid home in San Francisco." **GOAL** → "To make a living doing whatever I want to do; live in a bunch of places in Europe + America simultaneously; and smoke cloves w/out stomping on my lungs. I love cloves."

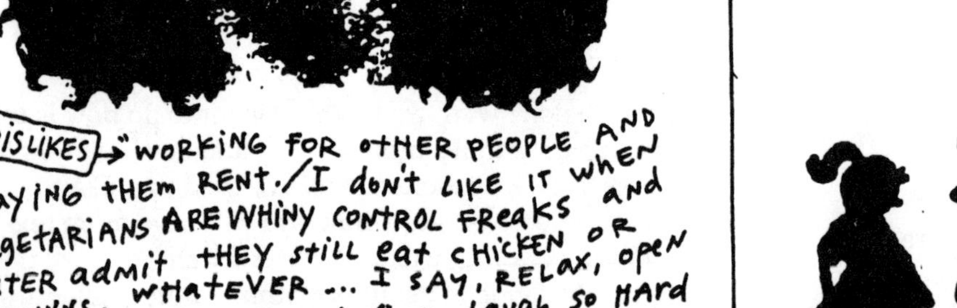

WHERE I'VE BEEN PUBLISHED (+ will be regularly published) "The book, GIRLFRIEND NUMBER ONE; 'PHILADELPHIA CITY PAPER'; 'F.A.D.' MAGAZINE; and now I regularly appear in 'THE SAN FRANCISCO BAY TIMES,' and soon in a new nat'l magazine published by KNIGHT-RIDDER, 'PULP,' AND THE NEW WEEKLY PUT OUT BY THE ANCHORAGE DAILY NEWS, '8.'"

ERIKA LOPEZ

THE Lopez STRAP-ON CARTOON

THIS IS NOT ABOUT WOMEN WHO PICK UP 1/2-FULL BOTTLES OF BEER W/THEIR LABIAS + DO HEADSTANDS. / NO. / THIS IS ABOUT OCCASIONAL BOUTS OF "PENIS ENVY" W/ "BREAST CONTENTMENT" AT THE SAME TIME.

STRAP-ONS ARE GOOD. YOU PUT ONE ON + YOU ARE IMMEDIATELY IN YOUR OWN SAFE, ANDROGYNOUS, K.d. lang KIND OF WORLD. / YOU WILL NOTICE A RUSH AS YOU FEEL LIKE WARREN BEATTY OR MR. "T," AND YOU WILL WANT YOUR OWN MONSTER TRUCK THAT YOU CAN FILL UP WITH ALL YOUR OWN SPERM.

TAKING PRIDE IN YOUR APPENDAGE, YOU HAVE FITTED THE HEAD OF IT W/ STEEL + NOW YOU'RE

MAKING HOLES ALL OVER THE BACK OF THAT BROWN RECLINER THAT SHINES... AND you're ON your WAY UP TO CHEAP FOAM SOFAS FROM IKEA WHEN NO ONE'S LOOKING.

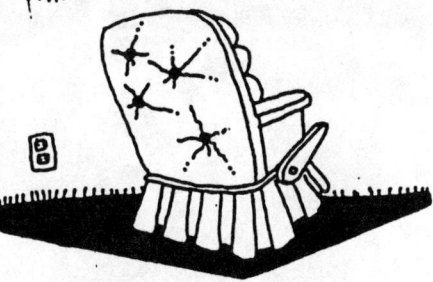

You later see yourself IN A BORIS VALLEJO FANTASY PAINTING W/ THE STRETCH-MARKS ON your BREASTS AIRBRUSHED AWAY...

AND NOW YOU'RE PROPELLED BACK BACK TO A TIME WHEN DWARVES LIVED IN CAVES, PYTHONS HAD OPINIONS THAT MATTERED + THEY COULD FLY, AND CONAN THE BARBARIAN WALKED THE EARTH... GIVING AWAY FRUIT.

"HI. GIVE ME FRUIT, CONAN, MY FRIEND."

"SURE, YOU SWEET PYTHON W/ OPINIONS THAT MATTER."

YOU'RE UNDEFEATABLE W/ YOUR STEEL-TIPPED VINYL STRAP-ON AND YOUR WELDED BRA...

YOU ARE DESIRED BY EVERY-ONE and EVERYTHING in THIS HOBBIT-INFESTED WORLD: MEN LUST AFTER you; WOMEN CRAVE you; DOGS AND ELVES DREAM ABOUT YOU; WHILE MOLLUSKS AND TROUT WOULD DIE FOR YOU. / YOU ARE RULER OF THIS WORLD.

THEN, LIKE A XXX PINNOCHIO, YOU FIND THAT IF YOU LIE, YOUR PENIS ACTUALLY GETS LONGER.

"YES. YOU ARE MOST DEFINITELY THE BEST Lover I HAVE EVER HAD."

Months later, YOU AWAKE TO A KAFKAESQUE NIGHTMARE: YOU HAVE FINALLY BECOME NOTHING BUT A HUGE PENIS W/OUT ARMS WHO CAN'T OPEN THE DOOR OF YOUR OWN BEDROOM. YOU EVENTUALLY JUMP OUT OF THE OPEN WINDOW, BUT A 1970's FEMINIST SEES YOU AND THROWS AN APPLE AT YOU. / IT IMBEDS ITSELF INTO WHAT USED TO BE YOUR BACK. IT FESTERS THERE FOR YEARS UNTIL YOU FINALLY DIE AS A LONELY, OLD PENIS SOMEWHERE IN MAINE.

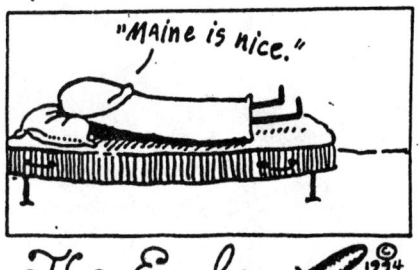

"Maine is nice."

The End.

© 1994 ERIKA LOPEZ

"WOMONSTRUAL"

BOOK REVIEW GONE AWRY

© 1994 by **ERIKA LOPEZ**

"Love the LABIAL Goddess with a FALLOPIAN-like LOVE"

I AM ANGRY AT TAMPONS + I DON'T WEAR THEM ANYMORE. IT'S NOT ONLY THAT I CAN'T AFFORD THEM, BUT I'M AGAINST PAYING CLOSE TO FIVE BUCKS FOR A BOX OF WHAT IS BASICALLY COMPRESSED TOILET PAPER.

These CORPORATE guys have REALLY GOT BLEEDING WOMEN BY THE OVARIES./ BLEEDING WOMEN IN WHITE STRETCH PANTS BY THE OVARIES:

"I FEEL CONFIDENT! AND YES, I'M WILLING TO DO CARTWHEELS IN PUBLIC!"

I WAS CONVINCED BY A BRA-LESS, EARTH-LOVING PRINTMAKER WHO LIVED ALONE W/ HER CAT, TO USE A SMALL SEA SPONGE. THE KIND THEY SOLD IN HEALTH FOOD STORES IN A SMALL FAKE VELVET POUCH.

Then while I was at THE HEALTH FOOD STORE, I BUMPED INTO A BOOK ABOUT WOMYN-STUFF. IT WAS POLITELY PRINTED IN SOY INK ON UNBLEACHED PAPER. IT WAS called:

Hygeia / A WOMAN'S HERBAL.

It was written in the 70s, AND I could hear JOAN BAEZ'S SONG, "Diamonds and Rust" as I turned the FIRST PAGE...

"On The Rag" and Other menstrual rituals -- for you, fertile sister

THAT's what the FIRST CHAPTER WAS CALLED. + BEING THE FERTILE SISTER THAT I WAS, I READ ON...

(I shall paraphrase)

"Do NOT BE ASHAMED OF YOUR BLOOD, OH SISTER.

I LOVE YOU, VAGINAL BLOOD. AND I AM NOT ASHAMED OF YOU.

DO NOT **HIDE** YOUR SOILED NAPKINS IN THE **DARK** TRASH. TAKE YOUR PROUD BLOOD TO THE AIR, THE **SUN**, THE **EARTH**.

Let GO OF THE EGG, AND SAY "Good bye, EGG"

And THE PAIN WILL BE EASIER. / DO NOT BE ASHAMED of bleeding.

PROCLAIM YOUR BLEEDING! YOUR FERTILENESS! LET THE WORLD KNOW/ AND BE PROUD! GET in touch w/ YOUR MENSTRUAL CONSCIOUSNESS

Squat over your HOUSEPLANTS THAT NEED minerals. AND DO NOT PLUG YOURSELF UP W/ WHITE PATERNAL PLUGS. BLEED FREELY AND MAKE YOUR OWN MENSTRUAL PAD. MAKE IT HUGE. / MAKE IT PROUD. A PROUD menstrual PAD, BECAUSE THERE IS AN ART TO BLEEDING.

RINSE! RECYCLE! DO NOT SUPPORT A HUGE POLLUTING INDUSTRY!

Maybe choose a purple FLANNEL TO REST NEXT TO your EARTHLY VAGINA.... AND applique a gold MANDALA on the front.... WHO SAID THAT EVERYTHING MUST BE WHITE LIKE THOSE HERMETICALLY SEALED TAMPONS + WEDDING DRESSES? **WHITE** MOCKS you FOR LIVING, EXISTING + SECRETING."

THAT WAS IT. THAT WAS ALL I NEEDED TO READ.

I PUT THE BOOK DOWN + WALKED AROUND MY APARTMENT CARRYING A SPIDER PLANT BETWEEN MY LEGS, AND SINGING SONGS ABOUT GERMAINE GREER.

MY CAT **FREAKED** OUT AND threatened to leave me forever if I didn't quit it./ But I WAS SO EXHAUSTED BY MY IRON DEFICIENCY, I DIDN'T HAVE THE STRENGTH TO TALK her out of it./ SHE WAS WALKING OUT THE DOOR + ALL I COULD SCREAM BEFORE PASSING OUT ON THE FLOOR WAS:

RINSE! RECYCLE! DO NOT SUPPORT A HUGE POLLUTING INDUSTRY!

AND A FEW DAYS LATER, AFTER I WAS RELEASED FROM the HOSPITAL, I DECIDED TO GIVE MY SPONGES A WHIRL.

I WAS PROUD AS I RINSED them in PUBLIC SINKS, JAMMING MY FOOT against THE BATHROOM DOOR./

I FELT SUPERIOR. SUPERIOR LIKE A SUPERIOR PERSON, IN BEING CONNECTED TO MY BLOOD / MY EGGS.

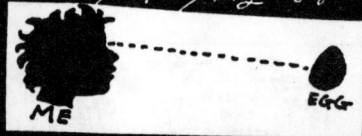

ME — — — EGG

I SAID "FAREWELL, MY LITTLE EGGS, FAREWELL" AS I SET MY BLOOD FREE, DOWN THE DRAIN. / LIKE A SAD BIRD-MOTHER OR SOMETHING.

I WALKED BACK INTO THE DENNY'S DINING ROOMS FEELING CONNECTED, IF NOT WAITED ON, AND I WAS AT A FEMALE Kind of Peace.

BECK MAIN

"A Baby Dyke's Progress" and "Square Peg in a Round Hole"
Kings Cross, Australia

Beck Main describes herself as "a neurotic Sagittarius WASP." She writes: "I was born in Perth, Western Australia, the most isolated city in the world, so I grew up with the Indian Ocean on one side, the desert on the other, and the enormous sky above.

"Camping in the desert as a kid, lying in my sleeping bag at night, staring at the sky made me get a thing about space, sputniks and astronauts.

"Fell in love with Janis Joplin at thirteen, and became a real out lesbian at eighteen. Fell in love with comics at thirteen, too, and have been drawing them ever since.

"Studied film at university in the mid-seventies. This made me realize how terrific comics are—you get an idea—and you draw it. With film, you spend years raising the money before you do anything.

"Had a dippy-hippy phase living in the country where sheep used to stare mildly at us through the lounge room windows. This made me a vegetarian.

"Is any of the above biography? Well, yes—it explains why the same things keep appearing in my comics—satellites, space capsules, beaches, lesbians, sheep, TV, alienation.

"I moved way across the desert to Sydney in the early eighties and since then, I've been paying for the big bad city life by working in a shop, painting and tracing in animation studios and doing illustrations."

Main co-published and edited *Drawing Away*, an Australian women's comic book.

Periodicals: *Lesbians on the Loose* (Sydney).

ANDREA NATALIE

"Stonewall Riots"
Guttenburg, New Jersey

Andrea Natalie was born in 1958, grew up in Arizona, and attended Cornell University. She then moved to Los Angeles, where she worked as a waitress, cab driver and janitor. In 1980, she moved to New York City and came out. She began drawing cartoons in 1989, inspired by folks like Lynda Barry and Gary Larson. Like Alison Bechdel, Andrea's work was first printed in *Womanews*. All three collections of Andrea's work remain in print. She's currently working on a fourth. Her "Stonewall Riots" cartoon is currently syndicated to twenty papers nationwide. In 1990, Natalie founded the Lesbian Cartoonists Network in order to encourage communication and support among lesbian cartoonists.

Books: *Stonewall Riots, The Night Audrey's Vibrator Spoke, Rubyfruit Mountain.*

Periodicals: *The Washington Blade, The Advocate, Common Lives/Lesbian Lives, off our backs, Gay Comics, Sojourner, Girljock.*

Collections: *Women's Glib, Women's Glibber: What Is This Thing Called Sex?, The Best Contemporary Women's Humor, Kitty Libber.*

STONEWALL RIOTS — BY ANDREA NATALIE

STONEWALL RIOTS — BY ANDREA NATALIE

AN INTERVIEW WITH ANDREA NATALIE

by Robin Bernstein

Robin Bernstein: Kris Kovick called you "Gary Larson on estrogen." Do you see yourself coming out of his tradition?

Andrea Natalie: Yeah, the tradition of Larson and Charles Addams and other single-panel cartoonists. I like to think of myself in the *New Yorker* tradition, more than Larson.

Robin: Were you influenced by underground comics or 'zines?

Andrea: When I first started syndicating, in 1989, I submitted to the undergrounds, but I didn't get much response. I'm a single panelist, and most comic books use a story format, so I didn't really fit in.

Robin: Which cartoonists do you admire?

Andrea: Among lesbians, I like Alison Bechdel. She broke ground for other dyke cartoonists. Some papers have to get used to running cartoons, and then their readership expects cartoons. And Alison was there first. Plus her work is beautifully drawn, and it's amusing. And it shows lesbians in a very realistic way. It's great to see ourselves in print.

Robin: You founded the Lesbian Cartoonists Network…

Andrea: In 1990. I didn't know any other cartoonists, lesbian or otherwise. I felt isolated, and I wasn't an artist—I didn't know what kind of pen to use, what kind of paper, how you syndicate. I wanted to speak with other cartoonists, so I started a network. Pretty quickly, there were forty people on the mailing list, and I published a little quarterly newsletter. Eventually, it became too time-consuming. Brandi Erisman, a Florida writer, took it over and kept it going for a while. Now Nikki Gosch runs it.

Robin: Let's talk about your first Stonewall Riots compilation. It was published by Venus Press, right?

Andrea: I founded Venus Press for the purpose of publishing the book; no one else would publish it. Once that book was out and it got good reviews and was nominated for a Lammy, I was able to interest several publishers in the second collection.

Robin: Why did you choose Cleis?

Andrea: Madwoman Press was interested, but Diane Benison had never published a book before. She was brand new; I wanted someone more established. Alyson Press wanted to eliminate all the editorial cartoons and just go with the humor. Sasha Alyson didn't think political humor was appropriate in a humor book. But I've always liked to mix it. And he couldn't give me a definite publishing date. He wanted me to draw fifty more cartoons; that was at the time of Desert Storm, and I'd done a lot of non-gay editorial cartoons that were really important to me. Cleis was willing to publish the book pretty much as-is, and I really liked dealing with Frédérique Delacoste.

Robin: Are you cartooning full time now?

Andrea: I cartoon more than I do anything else. I spent twelve hours sitting at my desk yesterday. But I don't earn my living that way; I'm a topless dancer.

Robin: You've only published one multi-panel cartoon—"Caretaker Blues" in *Wimmen's Comix #17*. Do you plan to do more multi-panel work?

Andrea: I would if I could interest an editor. I find *Wimmen's Comix* hard to break into. It's a small group of women in San Francisco who know each other and publish their own work. They don't really reach out. When I've submitted stuff, nine times out of ten, I've heard nothing. For the "Kvetch Issue," they included lesbians. The issue before that was called "Men" and I don't think they included any lesbians. Maybe one panel. And it had a very heterosexist introduction. The Lesbian Cartoonists Network really protested that. After that, they actually informed LCN what the topic for the next issue was, and gave us a chance to submit work, and some of us got in. Then, that outreach disappeared, and I didn't feel like pursuing it.

Robin: I don't think *Wimmen's Comix* has had an issue since #17.

Andrea: If they have, I'm not aware of it. They put out a big book about underground comics, *Twisted Sisters*, and didn't include any lesbian cartoonists, even though we've been very active in underground comics. Of all the stories, only one included lesbians, and it was about a woman who seduced a straight woman in order to lure her to a bar to make her girlfriend jealous. The conclusion is, the straight woman says, "Well! I guess it's not just men who are assholes!" There are like two panels worth of dykes in that whole book, and they're not really open to my material.

I really like doing my own books. I like doing solo work. I like doing my single panels, and I really think a comic book is not the appropriate place for them. *The New Yorker* is an appropriate place for them.

Robin: Your art has become a lot more detailed and precise over the years. Are you consciously pushing your art in any direction?

Andrea: No. In *Stonewall Riots*, there are characters that are close to stick figures; it's pretty crude, but I think the drawing has become more sophisticated because I've been doing it for five years. I think my own style is developing. I'm becoming more confident, using a felt-tipped pen a little more. One reviewer said a long time ago that my "scritchy-scratchy lines are like fingernails on a chalkboard." So I try to improve that.

Robin: You've taken on subjects that are controversial within the lesbian and gay community. You've criticized gays in the military and lesbians in AIDS activism, and you've done pro-S/M cartoons. What kind of reaction have you gotten?

Andrea: If there are reactions, I don't hear them much. There's the occasional letter to the editor. I don't get many letters.

Robin: So you've never gotten any backlash?

Andrea: No backlash, no attention. I wish.

Robin: Are you working on a new book?

Andrea: Yes. It may be called *Rumor Has It That You're Heterosexual*. It'll be my fourth book.

Robin: How many cartoons do you do a week?

Andrea: It completely varies. Yesterday I did three cartoons, but then sometimes I go weeks without doing one. Depends on if I have to go out and earn money. That takes time away from drawing. Plus, I'll be going to nursing school soon. I'm thirty-five, and you can't topless dance forever. I don't know how Alison Bechdel does it, but I find I can't make a living as a dyke cartoonist. She sells a lot more books than I do, and she does a lecture tour, which I'm not willing to do.

Robin: Why not?

Andrea: I like to draw cartoons; I don't like selling. And she merchandises. If someone wanted to merchandise my cartoons for me and pay me a royalty, that would be fine. But I can't take time away from the really important thing, which is the drawing.

Robin: Have you ever thought of creating on-going characters like Bechdel?

Andrea: Actually, I'm going to be doing a more mainstream cartoon, probably starting in a year or two. That may have a recognizable, recurring character or two. It's going to be a very silly single-panel cartoon. It's still in the formative stages.

JO NESBITT

Amsterdam, Holland

Born: Northumberland, England, 1949.

Education: Convent of the Sacred Heart Grammar School in Newcastle-upon-Tyne and University College in London.

Book: *The Great Escape Of Doreen Potts.*

Publications: *Sourcream, Spare Rib, New Statesman, Time Out, Feminist Review.*

Collection: *The Modern Compendium.*

How to eat melon in polite society:

a: the right method: →

b: the wrong method: →

.. two humourists on an evening off.....

BARBARY O'BRIEN

Middleton, South Australia

Barbary O'Brien writes: "I was born on a small island off the coast of England where I spent a lot of time drawing because there wasn't much else to do when it rained, which was often. When I was fourteen, my mother moved us all to an outer suburb of London to escape the isolation and to enjoy modern amenities like running water and electricity. I left school at eighteen, having failed Art, and got a job at McDonald's, where I managed to save enough money for an overland trip to India. When I returned, I had a go at finding a real job and became a computer operator at the London stock exchange. I stuck this out for three years, with a bit of voluntary community art thrown in—working with unemployed youth on an urban farm and painting murals in run-down housing estates. Finally, I gave up trying to be straight and respectable, swapped the flash job and corduroy skirts for a backpack and extensive world travel, and got a real education! This prepared me for life as a community artist in Australia, where I now live and work.

I specialize in working with young people, particularly those in jail or 'at risk.' Much of my work is geared towards education and communication and reflects my priorities of healing both people and planet, while having as much fun as possible. I now live away from the city in a small coastal community where I can draw cartoons in peace. I am embarking upon another collections of cartoons. I also paint and exhibit fairly frequently both in Australia and overseas."

Book: *Consequences*.

Collections: *What Is This Thing Called Sex?*, *Hysterical Women*.

Exhibits: *Trigger*, *Trigger on the Loose*.

MICHELLE RAU

"Lana's World" and "Lucky Rabbit's Reality"
San Francisco, California

Michele Rau published the feminist/lesbian cartoon 'zine, *Lana's World*, from 1989 to 1992, "because I loved what a confidence booster it was to see my own work in print, even if I had to do it myself." She was never that impressed with her own skills as an artist but believes that it isn't necessary to be a terrific artist to produce effective and funny cartoons, "Stick figures can be wonderfully expressive."

She continues to research fanzines and their history, a project she began as a graduate student in journalism from 1989 to 1992. She also publishes 'zines from time to time on topics ranging from dream journals to rodent trivia.

She writes: "I love to see women's anger and twisted fantasies in print. I believe that, to some degree, men's sense of humor is qualitatively different from women's sense of humor—women go more for the situational, personal, grounded-in-reality humor; they go for irony, subtlety, and quality. Men just don't understand women's sense of humor, so they claim that women don't have one (remind you of anything? like sexuality for example?). I don't believe that *all* creative work by lesbians has to have a lesbian theme. Riot Grrrls rule."

Periodicals: *Lana's World* (editor), *Lesbian Contradiction, Girljock, Factsheet 5, Holy Titclamps.*

Formative Influences: Saturday morning cartoons, Sunday funnies, Art Nouveau and Art Deco, white space, form follows function, absurdism and irony, *Nuclear Mutinous Dogs* skateboard 'zine, collage art, mail art, detournement, Aubrey Beardsley, Ken Brown, other artists whose work I've seen in 'zines.

Dislikes: Recycling trucks, the chronically clueless, bad drivers (the Anti-Destination League), world overpopulation, taxes.

Politics: Mostly far-left, lightly salted with far-right inconsistencies. Politically incorrect without guilt, I barbecue veal burgers with glee. Access to technology is a right, not a privilege.

Most Recent Accomplishment: Surviving a collision with a recycling truck (motorcycle accident).

Leisure Activities: Rodent Mom, cactus gardener, Internet inhabitant, crack shot with a .22 and motorcyclist.

Goals: Own Rau's Rodent Rehab Ranch in the desert, write a book about the history of fanzines, operate my own publishing company.

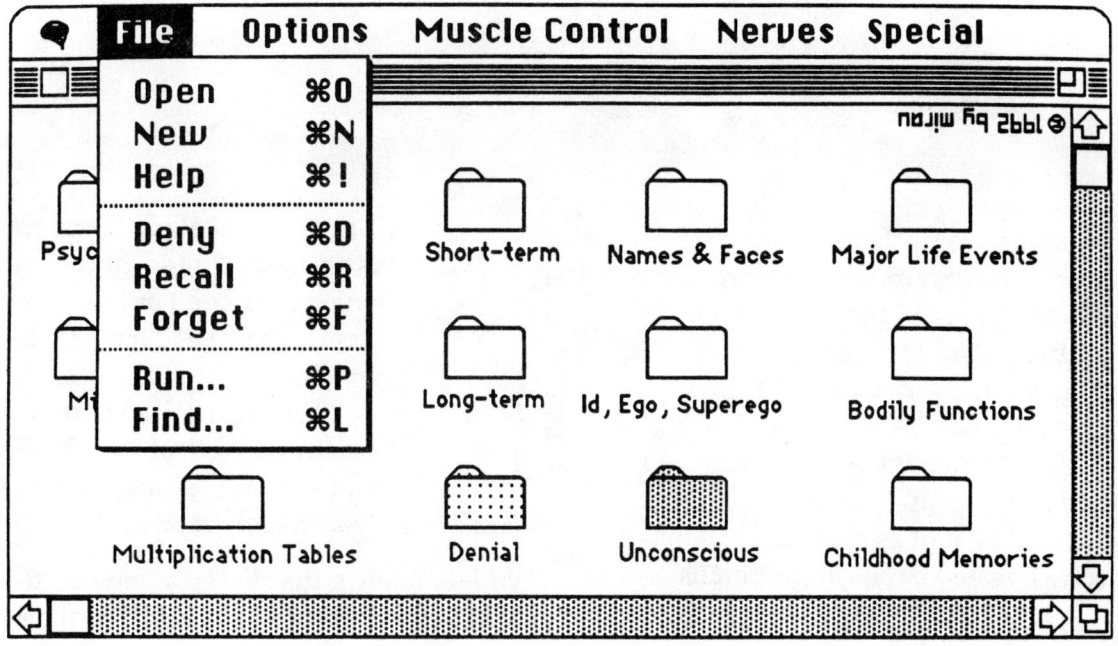

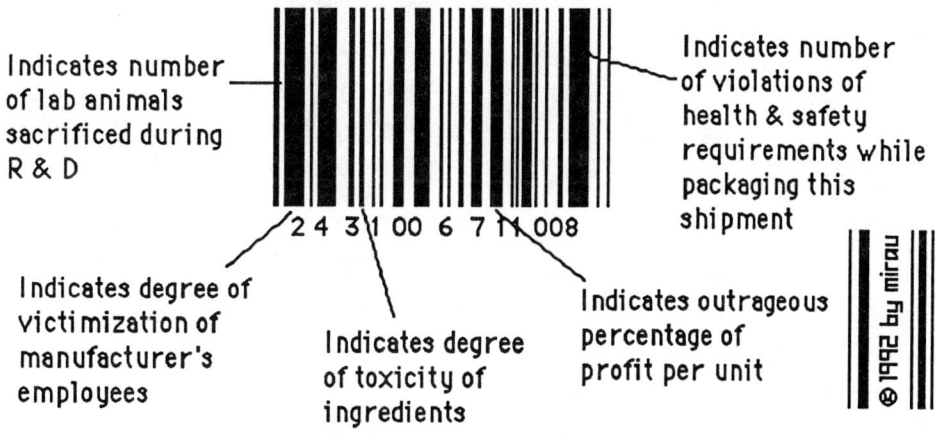

DIANNE REUM

"Tomboy"
Portland, Oregon

"Though I was raised in Portland, Oregon," writes Dianne Reum, "I still haven't totally grown up anywhere. In Grants Pass, Oregon, in the late sixties and early seventies, when my hormones were thumping into awareness, I noticed the girls who got the most attention were girls who had breasts. Some girls compensated for their lack of boobs by dressing and acting in a way society then thought of as particularly feminine. Others, still, compensated by becoming 'brains.'

"I had two fortes: sports, and humor. I loved sports (especially basketball) but when I was in junior high and high school, all sports money went to boys.

"This left humor, which was easy to cultivate since I came from a funny family, and we lived next door to a funny family. I had an artistic flair, but I developed it mainly by embellishing notes I passed, during classes, with self-caricatures.

"My mom painted in oils: big, splashy abstracts. When she sold one for a thousand dollars, I decided to concentrate on my artistic abilities. I began compiling a collection of serious pen and ink drawings. I surprised people (even myself) with my subject matter: in the beginning, all my renderings were of extremely sad people.

"Unfortunately, the demand for fine art in a small logging town in the seventies was probably about equal to the demand for Bic lighters in hell. To survive, I took typical small town jobs (restaurants, grocery stores, etc.) all the while working on my art. When someone approached me about painting a sign for their business, I discovered the world of commercial art, which didn't satisfy my soul, but it did please my stomach, since I actually got paid for work I'd done.

"While perusing a local Portland paper, *Just Out*, in late 1989, I saw an ad calling for cartoon submissions to be included in an anthology of women's humor. I put together a batch of cartoons titled 'Tomboy,' based on my childhood experiences, and used the caricature that had been with me since the sixties. Silverleaf Press bought all three, and I was immediately bitten by the cartooning bug. (It was, I might add, a 'love' bite.)

"I've found since that being a good cartoonist is not nearly as much about being a good artist as it is about being a good observer.

"Of course, being a lesbian influences my work because it influences my life and my viewpoints. Only in retrospect can I say that my early work was so depressing because internally I was in agony. I wasn't the same as the other girls, and I didn't know why. I didn't really know I was a homosexual, but I certainly knew I didn't want to be a 'queer' because that was a dirty word and, obviously, an ugly thing. (I was once slapped by my mother for using it as a dirty name.)

"I became, in many ways, an outsider. It looked rebellious (which was cool), but in the invisible ways. Being on the outside wasn't by choice, it hurt.

"Being in a book where I'm identified as a 'lesbian' is the biggest public risk I've ever taken.

"It's just plain time; I am who I am."

Book: *Tomboy.*

Periodicals: *Bluestocking* (Portland, Oregon), *Ms., Playgirl, Lesbian Contradiction, OH....*

Collections: *Women's Glibber, Kitty Libber: Cat Cartoons by Women, Mothers!: Cartoons by Women, What Is This Thing Called Sex?, The Best Contemporary Women's Humor, Weenietoons, Silverleaf's Choice.*

The most telling "Tomboy," which first appeared in OH... comics, was "The Crush." I don't have to say "Look, no one lured this girl into a gay lifestyle; it happened as innocently as it happens for any little boy or girl" because the reader has witnessed the way it happened. Seeing is the best way for most people to hear.

Barbara Findlen from Ms. asked me to come up with something about the Anita Hill hearings.

URSULA ROMA

I was born in Friendsville, Pennsylvania in 1963. I realized that I was kind of a freak at age 4, when I lathered up my face and shaved with my father's razor. It was Easter and I wanted to look good for the family. It seemed like the thing to do. I passed out from the loss of blood and my grandmother thought I was dead. Not quite. When I was seven my mom cut my long flowing mane of hair to a short pixie. The young dyke look. I felt bold and excited till my 2nd grade teacher cried when she saw it. This caused me to cry because I had  a crush on her. I also had crushes on my 3rd and 5th grade teachers, and of course on many friends.

Loved the night I woke up to find my friend from allstar softball caressing my entire body. This was a formative experience. It raised some questions, though, as to the butch-femme thing for me. She had a deep sexy voice, short haircut, and a very womanly body for a seventh grader. I was arousingly confused. Then at age 15, I kissed my best friend, and we proceeded to kiss for the next 4 years. This continuity helped. We deliberated about telling my Lesbian Aunt, but decided against it, in case there was some kind of evil plot to destroy our fabulous reputations.

In 1982 Art School beckoned. There I found millions of other sexual deviants, but managed to remain focused on my work. After getting a BFA, I moved to San Francisco, then to New York, but decided that both were too hip and livable, so I moved to Cincinnati - the gay mecca. I must force myself to have patience with surrounding bumperstickers, but otherwise this city provides many interesting ideas for my postcards. 8 years and 155 cards later, Little Bear Graphics is still thriving. My identity as a lesbian doesn't seem to present as many obstacles as the fact that I am a woman. This remains the basis for most of my humor. ■

They told her she was missing something upstairs.

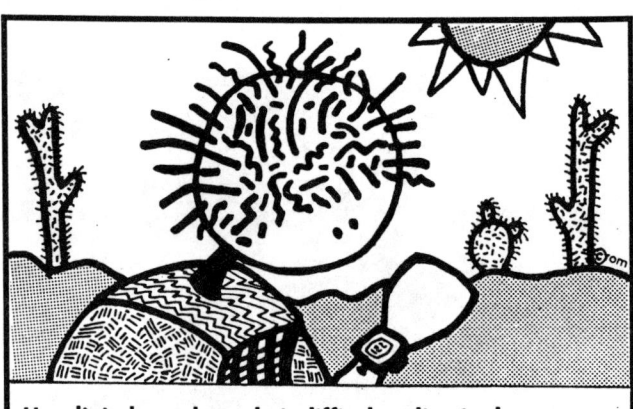
Her digital watch made it difficult to live in the moment.

She was overwhelmed by her thoughts.

Babes at breakfast.

Lesbians at lunch.

Dykes at dinner.

coffee queers

URSULA ROMA

It's hard to be nostalgic when you can't remember anything.

She had to draw the line somewhere.

Masturbation proved less painful after being declawed.

One thing in her life seemed constant.

She didn't want to miss a thing.

She was left to her own devices.

URSULA ROMA

CREATIVE/ARTISTIC INFLUENCES: Pop's humor, mom's creativity
PERSONAL/POLITICAL INFLUENCE: Being a lesbian.
DAY JOB: Freelance Designer & Illustrator
PROCRASTINATE: What?
MUSIC: Ella, Phoebe, Joni, Shawn, Indigo, Story
UNWIND: Deconstruct then reconstruct...my house.
PETS: Thelma & Ester - obviously mountain lions.
HOBBIES: Collecting dust. **INTERESTS:** Practicing my omnipotence.
PUBLISHED: Crossing Press - Women's Glib Calendar 1993 & 1994, Women's Glibber, Kitty Libber, What Is This Thing Called Sex?. Hotwire Magazine, Feminist Bookstore News, Lesbian Contradiction, The Radical Bookseller
ANYTHING ELSE: These are all self-portraits.

URSULA ROMA

NOREEN STEVENS

"The Chosen Family"
Winnipeg, Manitoba, Canada

Noreen Stevens is "a dyke cartoonist, visual artist and social activist living in Winnipeg, Manitoba, the queer geographical center of North America. She shares her home with her goldfish, Gill, and three juggling balls, all of whom she tries to manipulate and control, with varying degrees of success."

Noreen is one half (with photographer Sheila Spence) of Average Good Looks, a terrorist girl-gang of two, which creates queer-positive billboard and text images for display anywhere and everywhere. She cites the trauma of a suburban childhood as her source of strength and inspiration: "What I want to look at are the untold thousands of lesbians with one foot in the Land of White Bread and the other in a pair of Birkenstocks."

Stevens and Spence recently began another successful collaboration; in the summer of 1993, they (and three other women) opened Winona's. Noreen writes: "In January 1993, we'd noticed a tiny commercial vacancy near our homes and had commented on the need in our neighborhood for a cappuccino bar. I was inspired during our residency at the Banff Center for the Arts with the sense of community that had developed there. It was with that in mind that I tackled the notion of starting Winona's. We opened in July and it quickly became a gay/lesbian hangout, though not exclusively. This feels remarkable; a first in this city of 650,000—something besides a bar where alcohol is the focus. We welcome everyone to a space that has a notable gay/lesbian sensibility and they seem to like it."

Periodicals: Gay Comics, The Advocate.

Collections: The Best Contemporary Women's Humor, Women's Glibber, Weenietoons, A Queer Sense of Humor.

Cover Art and Illustrations: Can't Keep A Straight Face: A Lesbian Looks and Laughs at Life.

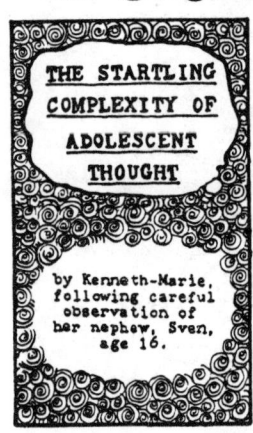

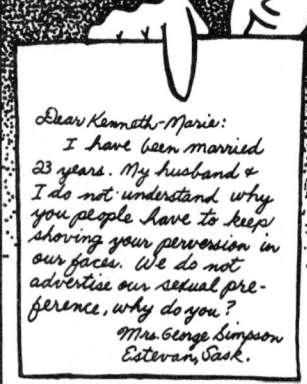

THE CHOSEN FAMILY

by Noreen Stevens

The Traumas of Butch Moms and their Children
by Noreen Stevens

1. "I don't think I'm doing this right..." / "I *told* you... divide the hair into **three** parts!!"

2. "Mom...this shirt don't have any buddons" / "*There* you go... good as **new**!!" / "Thanks, mom" *staple staple*

3. "*Alex*, the concert starts in twenty minutes" / "One sec... baby, your mom and I have a **bet** goin' on this game"

4. "I'm sorry Jimmy, I don't **have** a kleenex" / "Not even in your **purse**?"

5. "So, Anna...this must be your ♥ **Daddy**?!" / "Ma'am!?" / "Sort of!"

AN INTERVIEW WITH NOREEN STEVENS

by Naomi Guilbert

Naomi Guilbert: I know you've been cartooning since 1984. How are you currently supporting yourself?

Noreen Stevens: Right now, I have my own graphic design business and I do a lot of freelance graphic design and layout—mostly for clients in the women's community, the gay community, the arts community and the social services community. This work, combined with my cartooning, is where my income comes from. I have a degree in interior design which I've used only once, to design the women's bookstore here in Winnipeg.

Naomi: It seems that your degree hasn't really helped you that much in terms of your business and the direction in which it's developed. Has your university education helped your cartooning work in any way?

Noreen: I learned how to print neatly. [*Laughter*] Actually, university provided a good theoretical education in the field of design and so, in that way, it was good.

Naomi: Tell me a little about your family and your childhood. Is there anything about it that you consider pertinent to your cartooning?

Noreen: I had an interesting childhood because my parents were forty-eight and fifty when I was born, and they had two other children who were seventeen and twenty at the time. Growing up in that environment altered my perceptions of age and left me with first hand experience of different generational values—something that has helped with character development in my cartooning. I was also rather unexpected, and my birth—my whole existence— was something of an occasion to my family. For years, my mother thought I was a lesbian because she was so old when she had me. Now she thinks it's because she accidentally dropped me down the stairs.

Naomi: Are there any other lesbian cartoonists in Winnipeg that you know of?

Noreen: No.

Naomi: What about in central Canada?

Noreen: No—none in Canada.

Naomi: You don't know any other lesbian cartoonists in Canada?

Noreen: No.

Naomi: Can you talk a little about the isolation of being a cartoonist? [*Laughter*] For example, I think there is a lot of support for women who write. They can form writing groups. There are also conferences organized by writers' guilds and associations. Obviously, the situation is different for cartoonists. Where do you get your support?

Noreen: Andrea Natalie's effort to establish a Lesbian Cartoonists Network is going to prove vital for a lot of women. There's no one I can sit down and have coffee and talk about lesbian cartooning with. I've been corresponding with Alison Bechdel and with Andrea, but it's virtually impossible when you're corresponding with someone to really talk in any detail about what you're doing. What I've suggested to Andrea is an annual conference where the group of us could get together in one room and talk. I think that would be wonderful, although it would take a lot of time and a lot of money to organize.

Naomi: How has your lesbian identity impacted on your cartooning?

Noreen: Well, that kind of question is something that I wrestle with a lot because I don't know if I'm a gay cartoonist or just a cartoonist who is gay. I think I lean toward the latter. As far as the cartoons go, it's more a question of who the audience is than who I am. Most of the cartoons are published in the gay press, and the sense of humor has to appeal to that readership. There's a big part of me that would like to reach a broader audience. But it's a question of what audience is ready for some gay content in a cartoon, and I would never do it if it meant watering it down. If I could find some way to strike a balance between having gay content and appealing to a mainstream audience, I would move toward that. I still feel that I'm learning how to be a cartoonist. As I understand the process better, I can see a point in the future where I'll be able to conceive of something that will cross over into a wider market.

Naomi: Your cartoons are circulated to about fifty papers in Canada and the States and abroad—Australia, Britain, New Zealand, Ireland. What kind of responses have you been getting?

Noreen: The response has been overwhelmingly positive, and the criticisms have generally been very supportive— from people who are interested in what I'm doing, and who want to offer suggestions and push me toward refining and improving what I'm doing.

Naomi: There was one incident I remember you telling me

about involving *Kinesis*—a Vancouver women's paper—how they rejected your work because they felt it was insensitive. Another feminist writer I know has had similar problems—she's had work that was, in her view, a critique of pornography rejected on the grounds that it was pornographic. Do you think this happens often?

Noreen: It's only happened to me in this one situation, and I think I've probably been connected in some way over the years to maybe a hundred different publications. I think there are pockets in the feminist community, in the lesbian community, that are really driven by the concept of Political Correctness. And if, in a place like that, there's no leveling influence that challenges those ideas, you do get knee-jerk reactions. What made me angry about the situation with *Kinesis* was that I didn't feel the criticism was offered in a supportive way. It was cutting and judgmental. At the point at which they wrote to me, they had received sixteen cartoons. They singled out three of them and offered detailed criticism, and then, in conclusion, seemed to make a sweeping judgment about me as a cartoonist, and me as a political human being.

Naomi: What were some of their comments?

Noreen: With the cartoon "Patti Polls the People," they thought it could be perceived that I was being ageist. With the single panel about abusive relationships, they thought I was being trite. "Flip," I think was the word they used—that I was making light of abuse in lesbian relationships. With that one in particular, I was trying to encapsulate the potential for completely different perceptions about a single idea of violence. Is punching the wall abusive? There are people who would argue both sides of that.

Naomi: I actually felt that cartoon was doing the opposite of what *Kinesis* felt it was doing. It seemed to me that it was asking people to look carefully at their relationships because behavior that might not appear to be abusive might actually be abuse.

Noreen: And on the other hand, maybe it's not. But either way, be aware of it. And don't be fooled by thinking that because you're in a relationship with a woman, you're not potentially in an abusive relationship.

Naomi: Can you talk a little more about the financial aspect of submitting cartoons to publications?

Noreen: The ability to pay varies enormously from paper to paper. The whole attitude toward payment also varies, especially between the gay press and the women's or lesbian presses. The gay press seems to be more solvent and more locked into the idea that they pay for submissions. Women's and lesbian presses are often too small or too insolvent to be able to pay for submissions. And also politically, I think, they expect people to contribute work. That's just one aspect of our culture—that if we want to be involved and have our work published, we can make it available to those places and they'll give us a forum. There are also, I think, some unrealistic expectations about exclusivity. *Common Lives/Lesbian Lives* will not publish anything that appears anywhere else, which virtually excludes me because cartoons have to be widely distributed.

The bottom line is that I couldn't do what I'm doing if I wasn't making some money. I don't like to come across as though my primary purpose with my cartooning is to make a living, because it's not. To be the best cartoonist that I can be, I need to be honing that skill. It's actually three or four of the big gay papers like *Xtra* in Toronto and *Chicago Outlines* that carry me financially and allow me to make my work available to smaller presses who don't pay or who pay very little. Some send complimentary subscriptions, which is nice and which I consider payment. There's this tiny paper that comes out of Nelson, British Columbia called *Images,* which is a quarterly for women in the Kootenays. They made it clear right from the beginning that they weren't in a position to pay, but at the year-end when they had a little extra money they sent it to me. That kind of acknowledgment is important.

Naomi: Can you talk a little about the actual process of cartooning? How much time do you spend on a single cartoon?

Noreen: Usually I envision a scenario; there are graphics and writing conceptually in my head. Each written cartoon has to fit into the space that I have, so it seems easier to write first. Once I've gotten some kind of a written structure, I can think about what kind of images I want. Between getting up and checking what's on TV and making a big lunch and other kinds of dicking around, it takes about a day. Probably if I sat down and just did it, it would take two or three hours.

Naomi: Have you ever felt like you can't cartoon, or that it's really difficult? How do you deal with those times?

Noreen: Well, it certainly happens. I had a hard time working after my last relationship ended—like, how am I supposed to be funny now? But the humor in situations like that makes itself apparent quickly enough.

Naomi: Where do you get your material?

Noreen: Day to day life. Until recently, I focused on isolated scenarios from all over my life. I'm trying to shift a little bit now to creating a specific set of characters and some kind of a story line that has more continuity. I'd like to have a little more interconnectedness to the people and what's happening to them. Kenneth Marie (the central figure in "The Chosen Family") has recently taken on the job of caretaking in her apartment block. Hopefully, a community of characters is going to develop with that common thread.

Naomi: Are you presently caretaking in your apartment block?

Noreen: What a coincidence!

Naomi: I want to talk more about using your life in your work. I've found that I've struggled with the way in which my life turns up in my writing, regardless of how it's transformed in the process. How do you approach using your life and the lives of other people in your cartoons?

Noreen: Well, cartoons often deal with situations of conflict or embarrassing situations—funny, but embarrassing situations—that have happened to other people. And it's difficult to know what's appropriate to include and what impact cartoons like that are going to have on that particular individual. There are things that I know about people that aren't public knowledge, but if I want to say something about them in a cartoon, how do I protect their identities or their privacy, and should that even be a concern? A friend of mine has said to me that as soon as you put something down on paper, it becomes fiction. But in my community, it's not so fictional that people can't identify themselves.

Naomi: Have you had any response from people who have identified themselves in your work?

Noreen: Nothing negative. It's either a neutral response or a positive response.

Naomi: When I've seen myself in your cartoons, I've always laughed at them, even though some of the situations you've depicted were often traumatic at the time they were happening in my life.

Noreen: Yeah, I don't know how much of a concern it needs to be or should be. I know that, in general, I'm really sensitive to hurting people's feelings or saying things that are inappropriate about people, and I think that awareness crosses over into what I'm doing in my cartoons.

Naomi: Not long ago, a heated debate focusing on racism and writing was sparked by the Toronto Women's Press. What are your thoughts on the ways in which race representation and racism impact on your work?

Noreen: The whole question of racism was raised by a woman from *Diversity*, a magazine in Vancouver, who noted that all of the people in my cartoon strips seemed to be white middle-class women, and she wanted to know if I intended to become more inclusive. At the time she brought that up, I didn't really have an answer. I didn't feel like I had much to include that tackled issues of racism or ageism or anything outside of my white middle-class existence.

As I start to work toward developing a group of characters and serializing the strip a bit more, I've had to think about who these people are going to be and how I'm going to develop material that's pertinent to their particular identities. I don't really know the answer to that yet, although I've started to develop a framework. On the main floor of the apartment block, I've been thinking about having two businesses somewhat in conflict with each other—a Native food co-op and an immigrant butcher. I think the next step is doing some research, and that's an aspect of cartooning that I haven't really concerned myself with up to this point. I've written about what I know and I've drawn what I know.

The other thing I have to consider is whether it's even appropriate for me to become a voice for other people. Or does it make more sense for me to be a white middle-class cartoonist writing about my life? I don't know. Alison Bechdel seems to have tackled that issue quite successfully, but I have no idea how she did it. I find it hard to believe that her life in Minneapolis included the kind of racial diversity her cartoon strip displays. But maybe it did. Or maybe she just decided she was going to have black and Latina characters and researched what that would be like.

Naomi: Why do you cartoon?

Noreen: I think the whole reason why I rejected interior design as a profession was that it felt like really superficial work. It doesn't seem to make any enormous contribution to our social fabric. Part of the reason my graphic design work is for the specific clients I mentioned earlier is because there does seem to be a redeeming quality to it. It's promoting organizations or ideas that I hold to be important. I think my cartooning is a further extension of that. It allows me to throw out political and social ideas with humor. And I think humor really disarms a lot of people when it comes to sensitive subjects. It's a good vehicle for getting ideas across, for pointing out weakness, for playing around with people's self perceptions and their perceptions of the world.

T. O. SYLVESTER

(Sylvia Mollick and Terry Ryan)

San Francisco, California

Artist Sylvia Mollick and writer Terry Ryan (alias T.O. Sylvester) have been a cartooning team for eighteen years. Their weekly cartoon feature in the Review section of *The San Francisco Sunday Chronicle* has brought literate laughs to readers for the past decade. Their single-panel cartoons have also appeared in countless radical and mainstream venues, from *The Advocate* to the *Saturday Evening Post*.

Mollick and Ryan believe that any given cartoon can be improved by adding another chicken or two. Why chickens? "Originally," they explain, "the idea was to explore issues of working women—since hens *are* working women—but as time passed, the chickens developed full personalities that included many dimensions other than employment." They also feel that using animal characters in a humorous context makes it possible to explore animal rights issues and vegetarianism in a non-threatening way: "If you can identify with an animal cartoon character, you might eventually come to see animals as sentient beings with a right to be here on earth, unexploited."

Periodicals: *The San Francisco Chronicle, Mother Jones, Boy's Life, Prevention, The Advocate, Vegetarian Times, Ms., Gay Comics, Saturday Evening Post, Saturday Review, The San Francisco Bay Guardian.*

Collections: *Women's Glibber, Computer Comics, Comic Power in Early Emily Dickinson, Sound Ideas.*

Birthplace: Defiance, Ohio (Terry), New York City (Sylvia).

Creative/Artistic Influences: Lily Tomlin, Jane Wagner, Walt Kelly, Saul Steinberg, Walt Disney, George Booth, Sam Gross, Jack Ziegler, Matt Groening's "Life in Hell," Warner Brothers classic cartoons.

Leisure Activities: Sylvia is an avid reader of nonfiction and has always been interested in metaphysics and natural healing. Terry reads mysteries and detective fiction, jogs, collects fossils and lies on the couch looking remarkably lifelike.

Most Recent Accomplishment: The work of T.O. Sylvester was featured in an exhibit at the Cartoon Art Museum in San Francisco, February through March 1993.

Pets: Both are dog-lovers, but consider it inhumane to leash chickens.

Goals: Syndication and a collection of their work.

WHEN FAIRY TALES COLLIDE

Or I'll huff and I'll puff and I'll . . . Say, do I have the right address?

JACKIE URBANOVIC

"Balanced Statements" and "Over Coffee"

Minneapolis, Minnesota

Jackie Urbanovic writes: "My first love was comic books. My second was drawing stories. My third was movies from the thirties and forties. None of which is surprising, given that I grew up in an isolated area and spent a lot of time alone (reading my sister's comics) or with my mother (who also loved old movies).

"Storytelling was practiced as a high art by my Lithuanian grandpa, my Aunt Sophie and Uncle Stan, my mom and my cousins. Being shy, I fine-honed the art of being an audience. But I longed to tell stories also. So I told them on paper. I was known as the kid who drew good horses.

"That is the foundation of my art, my life. What was left, as I got older, was to find a way to make a living at it. My parents were very supportive and put me through art school. I spent seven years key lining, designing, and illustrating at full and part-time jobs before I realized I would have to freelance in order to have a chance at the good jobs.

"I've been freelancing as an illustrator for twelve years. If anyone had described the frustration and poverty that were to come with the first eight years, I would have run screaming from the room. Today, I'm glad I did not.

"My paying work extends from children's books and toys to advertising and corporate PR. My comic book art is my labor of love, my 'fine art.' This is where I speak about being lesbian, tell stories about my sweetheart, my home, my community.

"I'm forty-two and I still collect comics, trading cards and toys. I still love old movies, storytelling and my family."

Periodicals: *Women's Market Share, Wimmen's Comix.*

Comic Strips: "Over Coffee" ran for eighteen months in the *Minnesota Women's Press* in the early eighties; "Mother Goddess Funnies," which I co-created with writer Susie Day, ran for two years in *Equal Time.*

Collections: *Women's Glibber, Mothers!, In Stitches: A Patchwork of Feminist Humor and Satire, The Best Contemporary Women's Humor, Images of Omaha #1, Choices: A Pro-Choice Benefit Comic.*

Birthplace: Trenton, Michigan.

Influences: My family, Carl Barks (Uncle Scrooge, Donald Duck), Ronald Serle, George Herriman (Krazy Kat), Windsor McCay (Little Nemo), Maurice Sendak, Lynda Barry, Alison Bechdel, Art Spiegelman, Walt Kelly (Pogo), Whoopi Goldberg, Lily Tomlin, Alice Walker, Frida Kahlo, Diego Rivera, Lewis Carroll, Lucille Ball.

Leisure Activities: Going to the state fair, rummage sales/antique hunting, walking with my sweetheart and talking, biking, watching old movies, reading novels and comics, eating out with friends.

Most of the Jewish characters I see are Jewish only because they say "oy vey" and don't "do" Christmas. I wanted to write Jewish characters who were contemporary, who grappled with Jewish issues, who lived Jewishly and spoke out loud about it.

hot morning
© J.M. Urbanovic 1992

LINDA SUE WELCH

"Out Of The Darkness"
Nashville, Tennessee

Linda Sue Welch was born and raised in Kenosha, Wisconsin, and completed her higher education at the University of Wisconsin. She spent ten years as an assistant director of residential and judicial affairs at the University of Wisconsin and at Vanderbilt University. "Since I was a high profile, live-in professional responsible for Vanderbilt's freshman class," she says, "I was very closeted. That's where I developed my panels. They were very cathartic in my coming-out process." Welch even made a little booklet from some of her cartoons to give to people when she came out to them. "I'd say, 'Here are some visual aids to help you with this,'" she recalls, laughing. "It was a struggle then—but now I find it all quite amusing. As I got more comfortable and less angry—so did my work. My work is getting funnier—as do I."

Because she lives in the South, and often features African-American faces in her panels, people assume that Welch herself is black. She isn't. She had used mostly white faces in her work until an African-American friend, looking at a pamphlet cover Welch was designing, commented: "I don't see myself there." After that Welch consciously made an effort to bring diversity to her panels. "I may have gone a little overboard," she comments.

Welch's first publication was in 1991, in *Query*—Nashville's gay and lesbian weekly magazine. Response to her work has been positive. "I *have* received letters from angry fundamentalist Christians," Welch comments, "That inspired me to do some cartoons about 'Christian attitudes.'"

When Linda's work began appearing, Andrea Natalie wrote and asked her to join the Lesbian Cartoonists Network. "The Network put me in touch with other lesbian cartoonists," says Welch. "My first thought was that due to possible competition, no one would be helpful. But I've found just the opposite is true."

Because Welch uses her personal life and close friends as inspiration for her work, "my girlfriend and friends fear that I'll share personal information in my panels." But the artist is careful not to invade the privacy of the people she cares for: "I need to remember to amuse, not abuse, when I'm using real life situations in my work." Welch works at South Central Bell, where she designs ads for the Yellow Pages.

Periodicals: *Girljock, off our backs, Query* (Nashville), *New Voice*.

Collections: *A Queer Sense of Humor, Women's Glibber, What Is This Thing Called Sex?*

Formative Influences: MAD, *Dykes to Watch Out For*, Jennifer Camper's cartoons.

Recent Achievement: I finally saved enough money to buy a computer.

Leisure Activities: I spend a lot of time on my computer trying to figure out what it can do.

ZANA

Tucson, Arizona

Asked to describe herself, zana provides: "I'm Jewish-American, forty-eight. I live in the desert near Tucson with my lover, Debby Earthdaughter." Cartoons are not zana's primary form of expression, but she's had a special fondness for them, "since the days when I started the MAD-addicts' club at my junior high, and cartooned my younger sisters and our hamsters." Zana spent a number of years as a clerk-typist, microfilmer, political worker and journalist before becoming disabled in 1978: "I'm fatigued easily, but use my available work energy writing and drawing for lesbian and/or feminist publications." Her work on the subjects of disability rights and able-ism have educated and influenced many readers and other cartoonists as well. Lesbian land has long been a focus of zana's life and work; for the past fourteen years, she's been involved with Sister Homelands on Earth, a "wimin's land trust." "As far as I'm concerned, lesbian culture is the most exciting thing happening in the universe—but we're not perfect and being able to laugh at our foibles helps me deal with the hard parts."

Books: *herb womon.*

Periodicals: *Lesbian Contradiction, Dykes, Disability & Stuff, Women's Press, Maize, Common Lives/Lesbian Lives, Sagewoman, Hikane.*

Collections: *Women's Glib, Women's Glibber, Le Donne Ridono, Cats and Their Dykes.*

Creative Influences: Alison Bechdel, Jennifer Weston, Nicole Hollander, Tee Corinne, Diane DiMassa.

Personal Influences: It's impossible for me to single out a few of the huge number of wimin whose lives and work have influenced me, but most of them are involved in work against racism, for disability rights, and in building lesbian communities on land.

Leisure Activities/Interests: Reading, community living, food (growing, foraging, cooking, eating!)

ZORA

(Kirsten Zecher and Lori Priestley)

"Zora" and "Single Out Zora"

Santa Barbara, California

Kirsten Zecher and Lori Priestley are "co-creators, co-artists and co-conspirators dedicated to celebrating queer culture" through their cartoon, "Zora." Although it began as a multi-panel strip, "Zora" currently appears in both multi and single-panel formats. "We decided to diversify—into single panel—to be able to fit into smaller spaces, albeit slightly more political ones," her creators explain.

The difference between their ages (Lori is forty and Kirsten, twenty-six) and upbringing (Lori is Canadian, Kirsten is from Texas) help bring perspective and depth to their co-creation. So far, "Zora" is published mostly in the queer press, but her creators dream of crossing over into mainstream publications: "We're ready. We're just waiting for the Sunday comics to grow up." Their goal is national syndication for "Zora" by the year 2000.

Periodicals: *Zora, Deneuve, Dykespeak, Lesbian News, GLRC Bulletin* (Santa Barbara).

Also available: T-shirts, cards, notes.

Creative/Artistic Influences:

KZ: A doodling grandfather, my inner child.

LP: My inner neurosis, an obsolete college degree.

Both: Alison Bechdel, Lynda Barry, "Calvin and Hobbes."

Personal/Political Influences:

KZ: The rape crisis center where I volunteered and learned about women's power, both taken and asserted.

LP: The March on Washington 1993, where I marched with Kirsten and her mother for our right to be human.

Music Listened to While Working:

KZ: World Party, Cowboy Junkies.

LP: Mozart (even though I turned Kirsten on to both of the above).

What They Do to Unwind:

KZ: Draw. Clean house (just kidding).

LP: Paint and draw on photos.

Both: Too cute, but we run together and enjoy beach swims together.

Leisure Activities:

KZ: Mountain biking, tennis, photography, exploring new places.

LP: Attempting to mountain bike, tennis, photographing Kirsten photographing me, exploring new places.

These "Zora" cartoons were immaculately conceived by a call for mother/daughter-themed humor by Roz Warren, which coincided with a desire to add levity to Kirsten's coming out rite to her mother. We sketched our very first "Zora," "Mom Comes Out for a Visit," on the plane traveling to visit Kirsten's mother in New York. The coming out and visit went fine with only a few coughing spells (an attempt at deep breathing). Kirsten's mom got caught up in the cartoon once it was published; when she wasn't featured in the fourth cartoon, she demanded to know where her character went.

RESOURCES AND RECOMMENDED READING

BECHDEL, ALISON

Gay Comics #19, All Bechdel issue (395 Ninth Street/San Francisco, CA 94103)
Dykes to Watch Out For (Firebrand Books/141 The Commons/Ithaca, NY 14850)
More Dykes to Watch Out For (Firebrand)
New! Improved! Dykes to Watch Out For (Firebrand)
Dykes to Watch Out For: The Sequel (Firebrand)
Spawn of Dykes to Watch Out For (Firebrand)
Unnatural Dykes to Watch Out For (Firebrand)

BOCAGE, ANGELA

Real Girl #1–7 (Fantagraphics/7563 Lake City Way NE/Seattle, WA 98115)

CAMINOS, JANE

That's Ms. Bulldyke to You, Charlie! (Madwoman Press/POB 690/Northboro, MA 01532)

CAMPER, JENNIFER

Rude Girls and Dangerous Women (Laugh Lines Press/POB 259/Bala Cynwyd, PA 19004)

DEBOLD, KATHLEEN

Out For Office: Campaigning in the Gay Nineties (Gay & Lesbian Victory Fund/1012 14th Street NW, Suite 707/Washington, DC 20005)
Word Gaymes: 101 Puzzles with Lesbian and Gay Themes (Alyson Publications/40 Plympton Street/Boston, MA 02118)

DICKSION, RHONDA

Lesbian Survival Manual (The Naiad Press/POB 10543/Tallahassee, FL 32302/phone: 1-800-533-1973)
Stay Tooned (Naiad)

DIMASSA, DIANE

Hothead Paisan: Homicidal Lesbian Terrorist (book) (Cleis Press/POB 8933/Pittsburgh, PA 15221)
Hothead Paisan: Homicidal Lesbian Terrorist ('zine) (Giant Ass Publishing/POB 214/New Haven, CT 06502)

FISH

Brat Attack: The 'Zine for Leatherdykes and Other Bad Girls #1–5 (POB 40754/San Francisco, CA 94140-0754)

FLENNIKIN, SHARY (editor)

Seattle Laughs (Homestead Books/POB 31608/Seattle, WA 98103) Contains work by Ellen Forney and Roberta Gregory.

FORNEY, ELLEN

Tomato #1–2 (Starhead Comix/POB 30044/Seattle, Washington 98103)

FRANSON, LEANNE

Liliane, minicomics #1–20 (self-published: POB 274/SUCC. Place Du Parc/Montreal, Quebec, Canada H2W 2NB)

GREGORY, ROBERTA

A Bitch Is Born (Fantagraphics/7563 Lake City Way NE/Seattle, WA 98115)
Naughty Bits #1–14 (Fantagraphics)
Sheila and the Unicorn (self-published: POB 27438/Seattle, WA 98125)
Dynamite Damsels (self-published)
Winging It (self-published)
Artistic Licentiousness #1–2 (Starhead Comix/POB 30044/Seattle, WA 98125)

HARPER, JORJET

Lesbomania (New Victoria Publishers/POB 27/Norwich, VT 05055) Illustrated by Joan Hilty.

HILTY, JOAN

Immola and the Luna Legion (B Publications/POB 41030/Victoria, BC, Canada V84 2K0)

HYSTERICAL WOMEN COLLECTIVE

Hysterical Women: A Collection of 100 Australian Feminist Cartoons (Women's Electoral Lobby WA, Inc./POB 6091/East Perth, Western Australia 6892)

JACKSON, CATH

Visibly Vera (The Women's Press/34 Great Sutton Street/London, England EC1V 0DX)
Wonder Wimbin: Everyday Stories of Feminist Folk (Battle Axe Books/Jubilee House/Chapel Road/Hounslow, England TW3 1TX)

KAUFMAN, GLORIA

In Stitches: A Patchwork of Feminist Humor and Satire (Indiana University Press/601 North Morton Street/Bloomington, IN 47404)

KOVICK, KRIS

The Thing I Love about Lesbian Politics Is Arguing with People I Agree With (Alyson Publications/40 Plympton Street/Boston, MA 02118)

LISTER, MAUREEN and TUFANI, LUCIANA

Le Donne Ridono (Leggere Donna Centro Documentazione Donna de Ferrara/via Ticchioni, 38/144100 Ferrara)

MAIN, BECK

Drawing Away #1–5 (Australian) Includes work by Beck Main, Rona Chadwick and others.

NATALIE, ANDREA

Rubyfruit Mountain (Cleis Press/POB 8933/Pittsburgh, PA 15221)
The Night Audrey's Vibrator Spoke (Cleis)
Stonewall Riots (Venus Envy/7100 Boulevard East/Guttenburg, NJ 07093)

NESBITT, JO

The Modern Ladies' Compendium (Virago Press/Random House/20 Vauxhall Bridge Road/ London, England SWiV 2SA)

O'BRIEN, BARBARY

Consequences (Wakefield Press/POB 2266/Kent Town, South Australia 5071)

ORLEANS, ELLEN

Can't Keep A Straight Face: A Lesbian Looks and Laughs At Life (Laugh Lines Press/POB 259/Bala Cynwyd, PA 19004) Illustrated by Noreen Stevens.

QUEER PRESS COLLECTIVE

A Queer Sense of Humor (Queer Press Non-Profit Community Publishing/POB 485, Station P/Toronto, Ontario, Canada M5S 2T1)

RAU, MICHELLE

Lana's World (POB 460896/San Francisco, CA 94146)

REUM, DIANE

Tomboy (B Publications/POB 41030/Victoria, British Colombia, Canada V84 2KO)

ROBBINS, TRINA

A Century of Women Cartoonists (Kitchen Sink Press/320 Riverside Drive/Northampton, MA 01060)
Choices: A Pro-Choice Benefit Comic (Angry Isis Press)
Strip AIDS USA (Angry Isis)

TRIPTOW, ROBERT (editor)

Gay Comics (NAL/Plume 1989)

WARREN, ROZ (editor)

Women's Glib: A Collection of Women's Humor (The Crossing Press/POB 1048/Freedom, CA 95019/phone: 1-800-777-1048)
Women's Glibber: State-of-the-Art Women's Humor (Crossing)
The Best Contemporary Women's Humor (Crossing)
Kitty Libber: Cat Cartoons by Women (Crossing)
Mothers! Cartoons by Women (Crossing)
What Is This Thing Called Sex? (Crossing)
GLIBQUIPS (Crossing)
Weenietoons! (Laugh Lines Press/POB 259/Bala Cynwyd, PA 19004)

ZANA

herb womon (HCR #2/Box 850-398/Tucson, AZ 85735)

Other Recommended Periodicals and Comics

The Funny Times (2176 Lee Road/Cleveland Heights, OH 44118)
Gay Comics (395 Ninth Street/San Francisco, CA 94103)
Girljock (2060 Third Street/Berkeley, CA 94710)
Hysteria (POB 8593/Brewster Station/Bridgeport, CT 06605)
Lesbian Contradiction (584 Castro Street #263/San Francisco, CA 94114)
OH... (B Publications/POB 41030/Victoria, BC, Canada V8Y 2Ko)
On Our Backs (526 Castro Street/San Francisco, CA 94114)
Strange-Looking Exile #1–5 (Robert Kirby, ed./Giant Ass Publishing/POB 214/New Haven, CT 06502)

Organizations of Interest to Lesbian/Bi Cartoonists and Their Fans

THE LESBIAN CARTOONISTS NETWORK (c/o Nikki Gosch/POB 5237/Santa Cruz, CA 95063-5237)
FANNY: THE DIRECTORY OF COMIC STRIP ARTISTS, WRITERS AND CARTOONISTS (c/o Carol Bennett/Unit 6A, 10 Acklam Road/London, England W10 5QZ)

BOOKS FROM CLEIS PRESS

Sexual Politics

Good Sex: Real Stories from Real People, second edition, by Julia Hutton.
ISBN: 1-57344-001-9 29.95 CLOTH; 1-57344-000-0 14.95 PAPER.

The Good Vibrations Guide to Sex: How to Have Safe, Fun Sex in the '90s by Cathy Winks and Anne Semans.
ISBN: 0-939416-83-2 29.95; 0-939416-84-0 14.95 PAPER.

Madonnarama: Essays on Sex and Popular Culture edited by Lisa Frank and Paul Smith.
ISBN: 0-939416-72-7 24.95 CLOTH; 0-939416-71-9 9.95 PAPER.

Public Sex: The Culture of Radical Sex by Pat Califia.
ISBN: 0-939416-88-3 29.95 CLOTH; 0-939416-89-1 12.95 PAPER.

Sex Work: Writings by Women in the Sex Industry edited by Frédérique Delacoste and Priscilla Alexander.
ISBN: 0-939416-10-7 24.95 CLOTH; 0-939416-11-5 16.95 PAPER.

Susie Bright's Sexual Reality: A Virtual Sex World Reader by Susie Bright.
ISBN: 0-939416-58-1 24.95 CLOTH; 0-939416-59-X 9.95 PAPER.

Susie Bright's Sexwise by Susie Bright.
ISBN: 1-57344-003-5 24.95 CLOTH; 1-57344-002-7 10.95 PAPER.

Susie Sexpert's Lesbian Sex World by Susie Bright.
ISBN: 0-939416-34-4 24.95 CLOTH; 0-939416-35-2 9.95 PAPER.

Lesbian Studies

The Case of the Good-For-Nothing Girlfriend by Mabel Maney.
ISBN: 0-939416-90-5 24.95 CLOTH; 0-939416-91-3 10.95 PAPER.

The Case of the Not-So-Nice Nurse by Mabel Maney.
ISBN: 0-939416-75-1 24.95 CLOTH; 0-939416-76-X 9.95 PAPER.

Dagger: On Butch Women edited by Roxxie, Lily Burana, Linnea Due.
ISBN: 0-939416-81-6 29.95 CLOTH; 0-939416-82-4 14.95 PAPER.

Daughters of Darkness: Lesbian Vampire Stories edited by Pam Keesey.
ISBN: 0-939416-77-8 24.95 CLOTH; 0-939416-78-6 9.95 PAPER.

Different Daughters: A Book by Mothers of Lesbians edited by Louise Rafkin.
ISBN: 0-939416-12-3 21.95 CLOTH; 0-939416-13-1 9.95 PAPER.

Different Mothers: Sons & Daughters of Lesbians Talk About Their Lives edited by Louise Rafkin.
ISBN: 0-939416-40-9 24.95 CLOTH; 0-939416-41-7 9.95 PAPER.

Girlfriend Number One: Lesbian Life in the 90s edited by Robin Stevens.
ISBN: 0-939416-79-4 29.95 CLOTH; 0-939416-8 12.95 PAPER.

Hothead Paisan: Homicidal Lesbian Terrorist by Diane DiMassa.
ISBN: 0-939416-73-5 14.95 PAPER.

A Lesbian Love Advisor by Celeste West.
ISBN: 0-939416-27-1 24.95 CLOTH; 0-939416-26-3 9.95 PAPER.

More Serious Pleasure: Lesbian Erotic Stories and Poetry edited by the Sheba Collective.
ISBN: 0-939416-48-4 24.95 CLOTH; 0-939416-47-6 9.95 PAPER.

The Night Audrey's Vibrator Spoke: A Stonewall Riots Collection by Andrea Natalie.
ISBN: 0-939416-64-6 8.95 PAPER.

Queer and Pleasant Danger: Writing Out My Life by Louise Rafkin.
ISBN: 0-939416-60-3 24.95 CLOTH; 0-939416-61-1 9.95 PAPER.

Rubyfruit Mountain: A Stonewall Riots Collection by Andrea Natalie.
ISBN: 0-939416-74-3 9.95 PAPER.

Serious Pleasure: Lesbian Erotic Stories and Poetry edited by the Sheba Collective.
ISBN: 0-939416-46-8 24.95 CLOTH; 0-939416-45-X 9.95 PAPER.

Politics of Health

The Absence of the Dead Is Their Way of Appearing by Mary Winfrey Trautmann.
ISBN: 0-939416-04-2 8.95 PAPER.

Don't: A Woman's Word by Elly Danica.
ISBN: 0-939416-23-9 21.95 CLOTH; 0-939416-22-0 8.95 PAPER

1 in 3: Women with Cancer Confront an Epidemic edited by Judith Brady.
ISBN: 0-939416-50-6 24.95 CLOTH; 0-939416-49-2 10.95 PAPER.

Voices in the Night: Women Speaking About Incest edited by Toni A.H. McNaron and Yarrow Morgan.
ISBN: 0-939416-02-6 9.95 PAPER.

With the Power of Each Breath: A Disabled Women's Anthology edited by Susan Browne, Debra Connors and Nanci Stern.
ISBN: 0-939416-09-3 24.95 CLOTH; 0-939416-06-9 10.95 PAPER.

Reference

Putting Out: The Essential Publishing Resource Guide For Gay and Lesbian Writers, third edition, by Edisol W. Dotson.
ISBN: 0-939416-86-7 29.95 CLOTH; 0-939416-87-5 12.95 PAPER.

Fiction

Another Love by Erzsébet Galgóczi.
ISBN: 0-939416-52-2 24.95 CLOTH; 0-939416-51-4 8.95 PAPER.

Cosmopolis: Urban Stories by Women edited by Ines Rieder.
ISBN: 0-939416-36-0 24.95 CLOTH; 0-939416-37-9 9.95 PAPER.

Dirty Weekend: A Novel of Revenge by Helen Zahavi.
ISBN: 0-939416-85-9 10.95 PAPER.

A Forbidden Passion by Cristina Peri Rossi.
ISBN: 0-939416-64-0 24.95 CLOTH; 0-939416-68-9 9.95 PAPER.

Half a Revolution: Contemporary Fiction by Russian Women edited by Masha Gessen.
ISBN: 1-57344-007-8 $29.95 CLOTH; 1-57344-006-X $12.95 PAPER.

In the Garden of Dead Cars by Sybil Claiborne.
ISBN: 0-939416-65-4 24.95 CLOTH; 0-939416-66-2 9.95 PAPER.

Night Train To Mother by Ronit Lentin.
ISBN: 0-939416-29-8 24.95 CLOTH; 0-939416-28-X 9.95 PAPER.

Only Lawyers Dancing by Jan McKemmish.
ISBN: 0-939416-70-0 24.95 CLOTH; 0-939416-69-7 9.95 PAPER.

Unholy Alliances: New Women's Fiction edited by Louise Rafkin.
ISBN: 0-939416-14-X 21.95 CLOTH; 0-939416-15-8 9.95 PAPER.

The Wall by Marlen Haushofer.
ISBN: 0-939416-53-0 24.95 CLOTH; 0-939416-54-9 PAPER.

We Came All The Way from Cuba So You Could Dress Like This?: Stories by Achy Obejas.
ISBN: 0-939416-92-1 24.95 CLOTH; 0-939416-93-X 10.95 PAPER.

Latin America

The Little School: Tales of Disappearance and Survival in Argentina by Alicia Partnoy.
ISBN: 0-939416-08-5 21.95 CLOTH; 0-939416-07-7 9.95 PAPER.

Revenge of the Apple by Alicia Partnoy.
ISBN: 0-939416-62-X 24.95 CLOTH; 0-939416-63-8 8.95 PAPER.

You Can't Drown the Fire: Latin American Women Writing in Exile edited by Alicia Partnoy.
ISBN: 0-939416-16-6 24.95 CLOTH; 0-939416-17-4 9.95 PAPER.

Autobiography, Biography, Letters

Peggy Deery: An Irish Family at War by Nell McCafferty.
ISBN: 0-939416-38-7 24.95 CLOTH; 0-939416-39-5 9.95 PAPER.

The Shape of Red: Insider/Outsider Reflections by Ruth Hubbard and Margaret Randall.
ISBN: 0-939416-19-0 24.95 CLOTH; 0-939416-18-2 9.95 PAPER.

Women & Honor: Some Notes on Lying by Adrienne Rich.
ISBN: 0-939416-44-1 3.95 PAPER.

Animal Rights

And a Deer's Ear, Eagle's Song and Bear's Grace: Relationships Between Animals and Women edited by Theresa Corrigan and Stephanie T. Hoppe.
ISBN: 0-939416-38-7 24.95 CLOTH; 0-939416-39-5 9.95 PAPER.

With a Fly's Eye, Whale's Wit and Woman's Heart: Relationships Between Animals and Women edited by Theresa Corrigan and Stephanie T. Hoppe.
ISBN: 0-939416-24-7 24.95 CLOTH; 0-939416-25-5 9.95 PAPER.

Ordering information

Since 1980, Cleis Press has published progressive books by women. We welcome your order and will ship your books as quickly as possible. Individual orders must be prepaid (U.S. dollars only). Please add 15% shipping. PA residents add 6% sales tax. Mail orders to: Cleis Press, P.O. Box 8933, Pittsburgh PA 15221. MasterCard and Visa orders: include account number, exp. date, and signature. Fax your credit card order to (412) 937-1567. Or, phone us Monday through Friday, 9a.m.–5p.m. EST at (412) 937-1555.